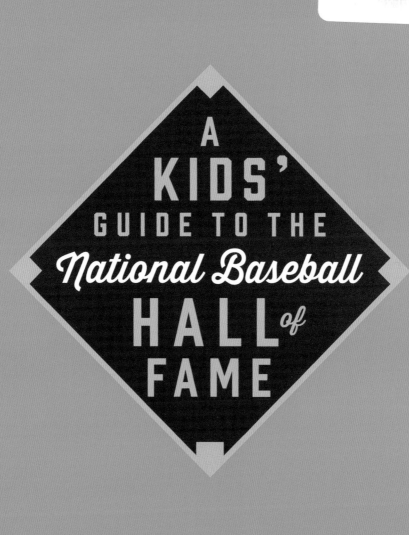

A KIDS'
GUIDE TO THE
*National Baseball*
HALL *of*
FAME

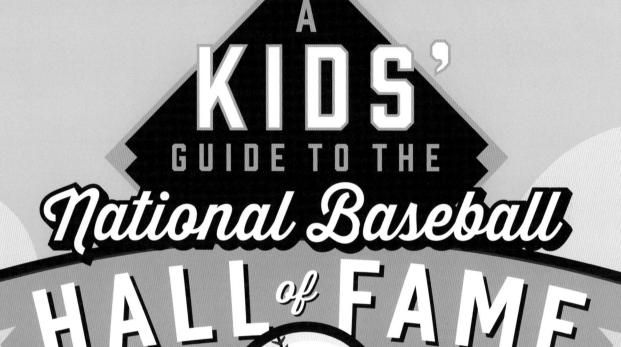

# A KIDS' GUIDE TO THE
## National Baseball
# HALL of FAME

The
**GREATEST PLAYERS** from **HANK AARON**
to **DEREK JETER** to **CY YOUNG**

## JAMES BUCKLEY JR.

becker&mayer! kids

# Contents

# Introduction

## MEET THE HALL OF FAMERS!

In a brick building in a small village in upstate New York, the Baseball Hall of Fame honors the game's greatest. Fans from around the world flock to Cooperstown, New York, to visit. With this book, you can take a trip to the Hall without leaving your home!

Earning a spot in the Hall of Fame is baseball's biggest honor. There have been more than 23,000 players in the game's long history—and only a tiny fraction were good enough to make it to Cooperstown. In this book, you'll meet fireballing pitchers, clutch hitters, speedy base stealers, and defensive wizards. Of course, some players are all of those things! From the mid-1800s to the latest Major League Baseball superstars, they're all in here, from Hank Aaron to Robin Yount. (Nope, no "Z" Hall of Famers . . . yet!)

### WHO'S IN THIS BOOK?

As of 2024, 346 people have been elected to the Baseball Hall of Fame. That includes players, managers, umpires, commissioners, and executives, as well as pioneers who worked off the field to help baseball grow. We've chosen about 180 of them to include in this book. You'll meet incredible stars from the 1800s and say hi to players you might have watched on TV . . . or in person! There is a short biography for each of these legends, but it's just a start. Make sure to visit the Hall of Fame's website (baseballhall.org) to find out more.

### ELECTING NEW MEMBERS

Since 1936, the Baseball Writers' Association of America (BBWAA) has played a big part in electing Hall of Fame members. People in the BBWAA vote each year for players who have been retired for at least five years. If a player gets

75 percent of the votes, they are in! Special committees also work to elect new Hall members. These groups focus on different times in baseball history, from all the way back to the 1800s to more recent decades. (More about the election process on page 140.)

(More about the election process on page 140.)

## LOTS OF LETTERS

With each player, you'll see their main position and the years they played. MLB stands for Major League Baseball. NNL stands for Negro Leagues. There were several Negro Leagues from 1920 to the 1950s. AL means the American League and NL means the National League.

### THE BIG DAY

Each summer, the new members of the Hall are the center of a weekend-long celebration in Cooperstown. The big event is the induction ceremony, during which the Hall of Fame officially welcomes its new members. Their plaque is revealed. They each also give a speech about their careers. If new members have passed away, a family member can speak for them.

### WHO'S NEXT?

Whenever you watch a Major League Baseball game, you might be seeing a future Hall of Famer. Look around at the sport today. Who do you think will end up in Cooperstown someday? New members are announced each December and January, so watch the news for updates. We hope your favorite players all make it to the Hall. Or, if you dream of playing ball, leading a team, or doing anything in the baseball world as an adult, you might end up there yourself someday!

## CAN YOU SPOT 'EM?

Watch for these three types of special entries:

WE'LL TAKE YOU BACK TO A KEY DAY IN BASEBALL HISTORY THAT FEATURES A HALL OF FAME MEMBER (OR MEMBERS!).

**BIG NUMBER**

WE HIGHLIGHT A KEY STAT FROM A HALL OF FAME CAREER.

NICKNAMES, BASEBALL SLANG, FUN QUOTES, AND MORE.

## HANK AARON ▶

**Right Field** | **NNL: 1951; MLB: 1954–1976**

"Hammerin' Hank" was one of the greatest all-around hitters in MLB history. He began his career with the Birmingham Black Barons in the Negro Leagues before moving to the Milwaukee Braves. He was the 1957 World Series NL MVP for the Braves and his 755 homers are the second-most ever. In 1974, as he broke Babe Ruth's record of 714, Hank faced down racist threats, becoming an inspiration to millions. Hank would go on to have a long career that included 25 All-Star Game selections and 2,297 RBI, the most in history. To honor this baseball legend, the top offensive player in each league now receives the Hank Aaron Award.

### MAGIC MOMENT

**April 8, 1974: As America watches, Hank Aaron blasts a home run to left field off Al Downing of the Dodgers. It is Aaron's 715th career longball, breaking a tie with Babe Ruth and making Aaron the game's all-time leader. As of 2024, he is still second all-time.**

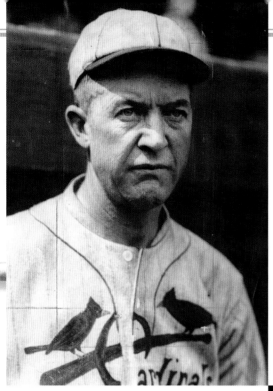

## ◀ GROVER CLEVELAND ALEXANDER

### Pitcher | MLB: 1911–1930

In the first half of his 20-year career, the pitcher known as "Pete" led the NL in wins six times and in ERA five times. Each of those five times, he had an ERA less than 2.00! Alexander led the league in complete games and innings until he finally became a World Series legend in 1926 with the Cardinals.

## ROBERTO ALOMAR ▶

### Second Base | MLB: 1988–2004

Alomar was the best second baseman of the 1990s, earning 12 straight All-Star selections and 10 Gold Gloves. A career .300 hitter, Alomar was the leader of a Toronto team that won back-to-back World Series in 1992 and 1993. He began his career with San Diego, but had his greatest success up north and in Cleveland, where he had some of his most successful offensive seasons.

## ◄ ADRIAN "CAP" ANSON
### First Base | MLB: 1871–1897

"Cap" wore many hats in the early days of the NL, leading the league's Chicago team as star, captain, and finally manager. He was the first player to reach 3,000 hits in a career, had .300-plus averages in 24 of his 27 seasons, and was also a manager for 21 years.

## LUIS APARICIO ►
### Shortstop | MLB: 1956–1973

Along with winning nine Gold Gloves and nine straight AL stolen-base titles, Aparicio was one of the first Spanish-speaking players to achieve national fame. Born in Venezuela, Aparicio was the 1956 Rookie of the Year with the White Sox and later a 13-time All-Star.

## LUKE APPLING ▶

**Shortstop** | **MLB: 1930-1950**

In 1936, Appling became the first shortstop to lead the AL in batting, and he did it again in 1943. By the time he retired in 1950, he held all career records for AL shortstops, including games played, assists, and putouts.

## ◀ RICHIE ASHBURN

**Center Field** | **MLB: 1948–1962**

If it was pitched, he could hit it. Ashburn won two NL batting titles with the Phillies and topped .300 nine times. If it was in the air, he could catch it. He led the NL nine times in putouts with his great speed and perfect timing.

## JEFF BAGWELL ▶

### First Base | MLB: 1991–2005

"Bags" could hit for power—he had nine seasons with 30 or more homers. He had an average of .300 for six seasons with a .297 career. And he had speed for a first baseman, stealing at least 15 bags five times. The 1994 NL MVP, he was part of Houston's famous "Killer Bs" lineup that included fellow Hall of Famer Craig Biggio.

## ◀ HAROLD BAINES

### Designated Hitter/Outfield
### MLB: 1980–2001

Over a long career with five teams (mostly with the White Sox), Baines was a dependable clutch hitter—more than half of his hits drove in runs for his teams. He began as an outfielder, but his bat made him into a top designated hitter (DH).

## FRANK "HOME RUN" BAKER ▶

### Third Base | MLB: 1908–1922

Hitting 11 homers in a season these days is not worth noticing. Hitting 11 homers in 1911, along with two more in that year's World Series, earned Baker his famous nickname. He led the AL four times in longballs for the Athletics and helped them in the Series in 1910, '11, and '13.

## IN OTHER WORDS

**Here are just a few of the popular slang terms (from yesterday and today) for a home run:**

| | | |
|---|---|---|
| Homer | Longball | Round-tripper |
| Blast | No-doubter | Grand salami (for a grand slam!) |
| Dinger | Yardball | |
| Gopher | Tater | |
| Jack | | |

## ◀ ERNIE BANKS

### First Base/Shortstop
### MLB: 1953–1971

Banks was a two-time MVP in 1958 and '59 for a last-place team, the Cubs, leading the NL in RBI twice. Banks was also known as "Mr. Cub" and was famous for his love of the game. One of his most famous sayings was, "Let's play two!"

## JAMES "COOL PAPA" BELL ▲

### Outfield | NNL: 1922–1946

"Cool Papa" got his famous nickname for his easygoing personality. He earned his way to the Hall of Fame with lightning speed on the basepaths and a .325 batting average. Satchel Paige used to say Bell could flip a switch on his bedroom wall and be asleep before the room got dark!

## ADRIAN BELTRÉ ▶

### Third Base | MLB: 1998–2018

In baseball history, there are only two infielders with five or more Gold Gloves and 3,000 career hits. Derek Jeter is one, and this late-blooming Hall of Famer is the other. Unlike many players, Beltré had his best years in his 30s, playing for the Texas Rangers. He led the league once each in homers, doubles, and hits, while playing lights-out defense.

## JOHNNY BENCH ▶

### Catcher | MLB: 1967–1983

Bench was the first catcher to show how the hinged mitt (which improved on the old pillow style) could work. Bench's strong arm and pitch-snagging abilities were legendary, making him an all-around superstar. No catchers since have combined his defensive excellence with as much slugging power. During his time, Bench was the Rookie of the Year (1968), NL MVP (1970 and 1972), and World Series MVP (1976), and he earned 10 Gold Gloves.

**October 8, 1956: Yogi Berra catches the final strike of Don Larsen's perfect game for the Yankees in Game 5 of the World Series. It is still the only perfect game thrown in the Fall Classic (that's a nickname for the World Series, always held in the fall).**

## LAWRENCE ◀ "YOGI" BERRA

### Catcher | MLB: 1946–1965

Sure, Lawrence Berra had a fun nickname, but he's in this book for one reason: his outstanding play. No player won more World Series games or had more World Series hits than Berra. He helped the Yankees win 10 World Series titles and won three AL MVP awards along the way.

## CRAIG BIGGIO ▶

### Second Base/Catcher | MLB: 1988–2007

Biggio was good enough at second to earn four Gold Gloves. He even stole base 50 times in 1998 and his 668 doubles—among his 3,060 career hits—are the second-most ever by a right-handed batter. He was also good at getting hit by pitches (see Big Number).

## BIG NUMBER

### 285

**The modern-day record for being hit by pitches, held by Craig Biggio. Ouch!**

## ◀ BERT BLYLEVEN

### Pitcher | MLB: 1970–1992

Curveball specialist Blyleven came all the way from the Netherlands to make it into the Hall of Fame, the first person from that country to do so! He was just 19 in 1970 when he pitched his first full season, winning 10 games for the Twins. After two years with Texas, he joined Pittsburgh and won a game in the Pirates' World Series triumph, then got his second Fall Classic win back with Minnesota in 1987.

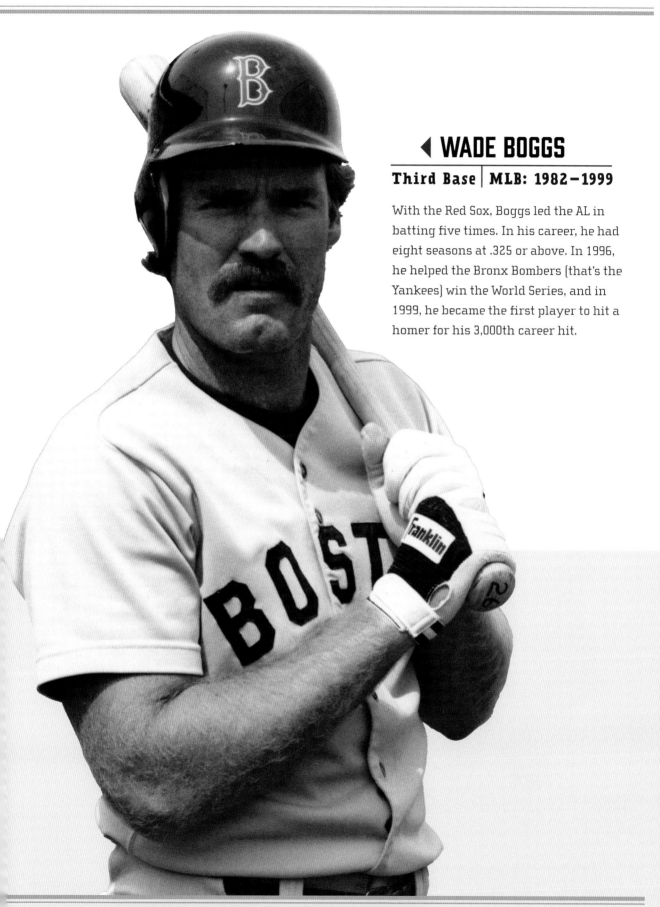

## ◀ WADE BOGGS

### Third Base │ MLB: 1982–1999

With the Red Sox, Boggs led the AL in batting five times. In his career, he had eight seasons at .325 or above. In 1996, he helped the Bronx Bombers (that's the Yankees) win the World Series, and in 1999, he became the first player to hit a homer for his 3,000th career hit.

## LOU BOUDREAU ▶

**Shortstop | MLB: 1938–1952**

As a two-time All-Star shortstop in his fifth season, Boudreau boldly asked to take over as the Indians' manager in 1942. And he got the job! At just 24, he was the youngest person to start a season as a manager. He also continued playing, earning a 1944 AL batting title and a 1948 AL MVP award while batting .355. He led Cleveland to the 1948 World Series championship.

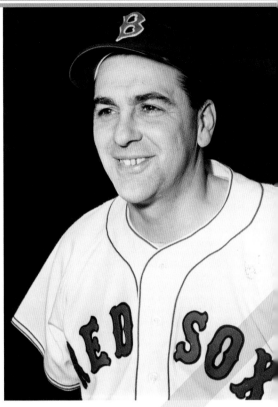

## ◀ ROGER BRESNAHAN

**Catcher | MLB: 1897, 1900–1915**

Bresnahan helped the New York Giants win the World Series in 1905. In 1907, he made his biggest mark by being the first catcher to wear shin guards! Bresnahan was also a player-manager later in his career.

## GEORGE BRETT ▶
### Third Base │ MLB: 1973–1993

Brett was one of the top hitters in the late
1900s. He won batting titles in 1976, 1980, and
1990, and he won three AL slugging percentage
titles. Brett was the first player ever to reach
3,000 hits, 300 homers, 600 doubles, 100 triples,
1,500 RBI, and 200 steals in a career.

## LOU BROCK ▶
### Left Field │ MLB: 1961–1979

Before Rickey Henderson (page 58),
Lou Brock was baseball's stolen-
base king. He retired with a record
938 steals and his 118 swipes in
1974 were a single-season best. In
three World Series, he hit .391 and
helped the Cardinals win the title
in 1964 and 1967.

8. DAN BROUTHERS

## ◀ DAN BROUTHERS
### First Base | MLB: 1879–1904

"Big Dan" was Babe Ruth before Ruth was born. He led the NL in slugging percentage from 1881 through 1886 and also led in homers twice. His single-season high was just 14, but things were different back then. Through 1888, he had hit enough to be baseball's career leader.

## MORDECAI BROWN ▶
### Pitcher | MLB: 1903–1916

Brown might be better known by his famous nickname, "Three-Finger," which he got thanks to a farm accident when he was a kid. But he was also an amazing pitcher, who helped the Cubs win two World Series. His disability informed his pitching abilities, giving him movement on the ball unlike any other pitcher.

## ◀ RAY BROWN
### Pitcher | NNL: 1931–1945

Brown had every pitch you could imagine. Along with Satchel Paige, he was one of the best Negro Leagues pitchers. He helped the Homestead Grays win eight pennants in nine seasons. Brown was a six-time league leader in wins, and in the postseason he had a 1.32 ERA.

## JIM BUNNING ▲
### Pitcher | MLB: 1955–1971

Bunning was the first pitcher to win 100 games in each league, starting for the Tigers and later the Phillies. He even pitched a perfect game on Father's Day in 1964, and it became a career highlight for one of the best pitchers in the 1960s.

## JESSE C. BURKETT ▶
### Left Field | MLB: 1890–1905

Burkett was a wonder at the plate. He had a .400 batting average twice and finished his career in 1905 with a .338 lifetime average. His bunting skills were unmatched and he stole 25 or more bases nine times.

# BROADCASTERS

**S**ince 1978, the Hall of Fame has honored the people whose voices tell the story of the game: radio and TV broadcasters. Their talents have helped millions of people experience every pitch, every hit, and every dramatic moment. Each summer, the Hall of Fame presents one of them with the Ford C. Frick Award for baseball broadcasting excellence. More than 45 people have earned the honor; here are some of them.

**RED BARBER (1978):** The "Ol' Redhead" covered the Brooklyn Dodgers and New York Yankees for more than 30 years. He was in what he called "the catbird seat" for those teams' great runs in the 1940s and 1950s. (Catbirds are famous for often sitting highest up in a tree full of birds. Announcers sit high above the field to call the games.)

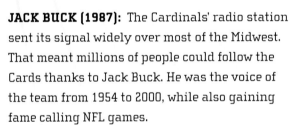

**JACK BUCK (1987):** The Cardinals' radio station sent its signal widely over most of the Midwest. That meant millions of people could follow the Cards thanks to Jack Buck. He was the voice of the team from 1954 to 2000, while also gaining fame calling NFL games.

**HARRY CARAY (1989):** Caray spent more than 50 years calling ball games. He was most famous for his work with the Chicago Cubs. He would sometimes call games from the bleachers, and often led the crowd in singing "Take Me Out to the Ballgame."

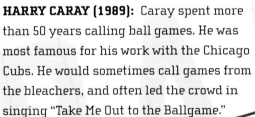

**BOB COSTAS (2018):** Instead of covering one team for most of his career, Costas covered all of them. He was NBC's national baseball voice for decades, covering dozens of important games. When he wasn't at a diamond, he was a famous voice on NFL and Olympic broadcasts, too.

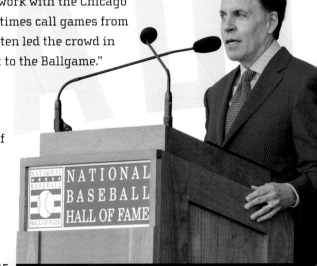

**JAIME JARRÍN (1998):** The voice of the LA Dodgers in Spanish for more than 60 years, Jarrín helped generations of Spanish speakers fall in love with baseball and Dodger blue. Jarrín also inspired and helped train dozens of other announcers; today, most MLB teams broadcast at least some games in Spanish.

**TIM McCARVER (2012):** His long-playing career (21 seasons with four teams) helped make McCarver a real "insider." He called games for many teams but gained the most fame for his national network broadcasts.

**JON MILLER (2010):** Several big-league teams, including the Red Sox, Orioles, and his hometown Giants, have enjoyed Miller's funny and fact-packed work. He also did the ESPN national Sunday night game for more than 20 years.

**VIN SCULLY (1982):** No one called more baseball games than the beloved Scully, who was on the mic for the Dodgers from 1950 to 2016. That's an incredible 66 seasons!

**BOB UECKER (2003):** After six seasons in the majors, Uecker started calling Milwaukee Brewers games in 1971. Through 2023, he hasn't stopped! His humor and cheer helped him have a career as an actor as well.

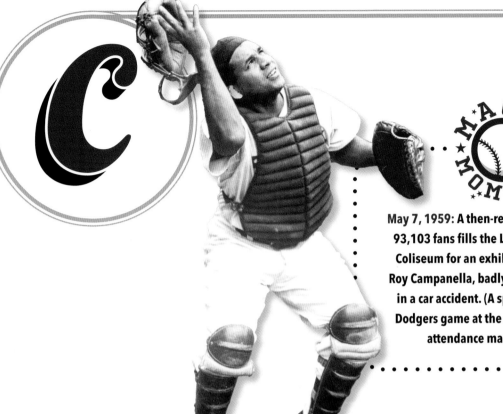

# C

### MAGIC MOMENT

May 7, 1959: A then-record baseball crowd of 93,103 fans fills the Los Angeles Memorial Coliseum for an exhibition game to honor Roy Campanella, badly injured a year earlier in a car accident. (A special 2008 Red Sox-Dodgers game at the Coliseum topped the attendance mark at 115,301.)

## ROY CAMPANELLA ▲

### Catcher | NNL: 1937–1945; MLB: 1948–1957

"Campy" was playing in the International League when Jackie Robinson broke white major league baseball's racial barrier in 1947. The young catcher soon followed Robinson to the Dodgers and became an eight-time NL All-Star and three-time NL MVP.

## ROD CAREW ▶

### Second Base | MLB: 1967–1985

Carew was a native of Panama who won seven AL batting titles, as well as the 1967 AL Rookie of the Year and 1977 AL MVP. He was an All-Star for 18 years in a row and is also a member of the 3,000-hit club, with 3,053.

## STEVE CARLTON ▶

**Pitcher** | **MLB: 1965–1988**

Carlton's awesome curveball and wicked fastball
made him a 329-game winner, four-time Cy Young
Award winner, and 10-time All-Star. He got his
World Series ring in 1980, winning two games as
the Phillies beat the Royals.

### ◀ GARY CARTER
#### Catcher | MLB: 1974–1992

Carter was among the top defensive catchers of his time, and one of the best hitters, too. Popular with fans, he was elected to 11 All-Star teams and was twice the All-Star Game MVP. He also helped the Mets win the 1986 World Series.

### ORLANDO CEPEDA ▶
#### First Base | MLB: 1958–1974

Cepeda played for six teams in his 17-year career after coming to the big leagues from Puerto Rico. First, he won the 1958 NL Rookie of the Year with the San Francisco Giants. Then, he was the 1967 NL MVP and 1967 World Series champ with the Cardinals.

# OSCAR CHARLESTON ▲
## Outfield | NNL: 1920–1941

Experts who have studied the Negro Leagues point to Charleston as perhaps the best all-around player. A speedy outfielder, he was also a tremendous hitter. His career average of .365 is second all-time. He led his league in RBI four times and in homers five. Charleston was also a manager for 14 seasons, some while playing at the same time!

## JACK CHESBRO ▶
### Pitcher | MLB: 1899–1909

Hundreds of pitchers have put together great seasons since 1904, but none have matched Jack Chesbro's 41-win mark that season. The spitballer not only won, he finished what he started for the New York Highlanders (as the Yankees were known then). He threw 48 complete games that season, more than today's pitchers could do in two careers.

## ◀ ROBERTO CLEMENTE
### Right Field | MLB: 1955–1972

Born in Puerto Rico, Clemente became a star with the Pittsburgh Pirates. His .314 average helped them win the 1960 World Series. He was later the 1966 NL MVP and a four-time batting champ with 12 Gold Gloves. In honor of Clemente's work as a community leader, Major League Baseball gives the Roberto Clemente Award each season to a player who has been a star on and off the field.

## TY COBB ▲

### Center Field | MLB: 1905–1928

When the Hall of Fame elected its first players, Cobb got the most votes. His career average of .366 is still the highest ever, more than a century after he played. He won 12 AL batting titles and retired with 897 stolen bases, still the fourth-most ever.

## " IN OTHER " WORDS

**Ty Cobb was sometimes called the "Georgia Peach." Here are some other memorable Hall of Famers' nicknames:**

- Big Train (Walter Johnson)
- Big Unit (Randy Johnson)
- Crime Dog (Fred McGriff)
- The Flying Dutchman (Honus Wagner)
- Mr. Cub (Ernie Banks)
- The Say-Hey Kid (Willie Mays)
- The Splendid Splinter (Ted Williams)
- The Yankee Clipper (Joe DiMaggio)

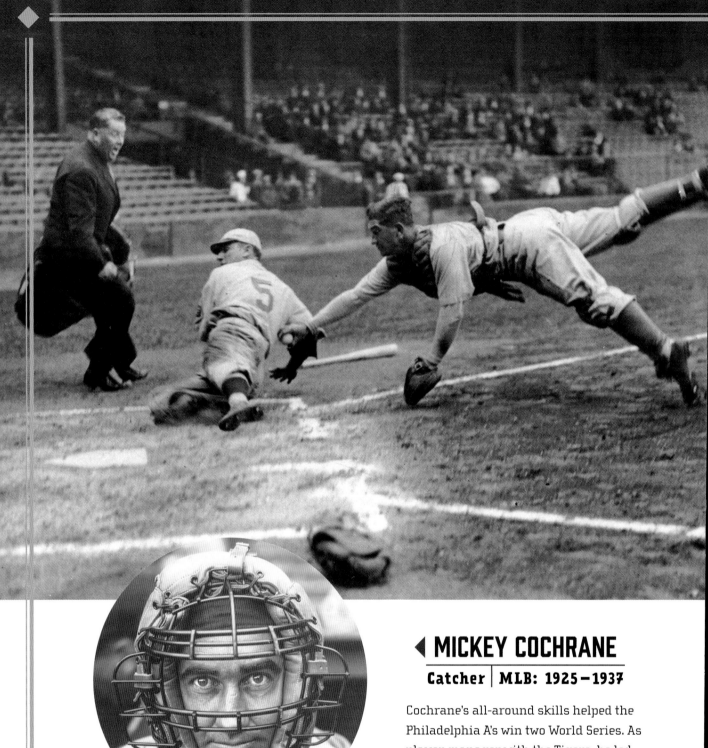

## ◀ MICKEY COCHRANE
### Catcher | MLB: 1925–1937

Cochrane's all-around skills helped the Philadelphia A's win two World Series. As player-manager with the Tigers, he led them to the 1935 Series title. His .320 career batting average is one of the best all-time among catchers.

## EDDIE COLLINS ▶

**Second Base | MLB: 1906–1930**

Collins had 19 seasons with an average above .300—and in 14 of those, he topped .325! Collins led the AL four times in steals; his career total of 741 is the eighth-most all-time. As for winning, he won three World Series with the Athletics and another with the White Sox!

## ◀ JOE CRONIN

**Shortstop | MLB: 1926–1945**

Cronin was a .301 career hitter and an excellent fielder with the Washington Senators and Boston Red Sox. But the seven-time All-Star is probably better known for being Boston's player-manager from 1933 to 1945.

# COMMISSIONERS

**S**ince 1920, the person in charge of major league baseball has been the commissioner. Chosen by team owners, the commissioner runs the business of the game off the field. Some commissioners have contributed a lot to the game—and earned a spot in the Hall of Fame! They are listed here with the years they held the top job.

**KENESAW MOUNTAIN LANDIS (1921–1944):**
The first commissioner was hired to "clean up" baseball after a betting scandal in 1919. He set the standard of the commissioner having the final say on most baseball issues.

**FORD FRICK (1951–1965):**
Frick was a longtime sportswriter who became the NL president. While in that job, he helped create the Baseball Hall of Fame. As commissioner, he was in charge of baseball's first expansion in the early 1960s, when baseball added many new teams.

### BOWIE KUHN (1969–1984):

Kuhn's skill as a lawyer helped him deal with a lot of labor issues while he was commissioner. It was a time when players were calling for—and getting—more rights to choose where they played.

### BUD SELIG (1998–2015):

Selig was a longtime team executive and owner of the Milwaukee Brewers. Major League Baseball grew a lot under Selig, adding more playoffs and interleague play.

## RAY DANDRIDGE ▶

### Third Base | NNL: 1933–1944

Dandridge starred for several Negro League teams as well as teams in the Mexican League. He was one of the best defensive third basemen ever, with a rocket arm and great range. He could also hit well, posting a .319 career average during Negro Leagues play.

## ◀ ANDRE DAWSON

### Outfield | MLB: 1976–1996

Nicknamed "The Hawk," Dawson is one of only five players with 400 homers and 300 steals. The 1987 NL MVP with the Cubs, Dawson was also a great fielder, winning eight Gold Gloves. Few runners dared to challenge his powerful throwing arm from right field.

## DIZZY DEAN ▲

### Pitcher | MLB: 1930–1947

Jay Hanna Dean got his famous nickname fo his slightly goofy personality. He led the NL twice in wins and four times in Ks (strikeout including both in 1934, when he helped the Cardinals win the World Series. Dean later gained fame as a popular radio announcer.

## ◀ ED DELAHANTY
### Outfield | MLB: 1888–1903

Average: Check! Delahanty's .346 career mark (including three .400-plus seasons) is still the eighth best ever. Power: Check! In an 1896 game, he was only the second player with four homers in a game.

## BILL DICKEY ▶
### Catcher | MLB: 1928–1946

Bill Dickey was the second catcher to wear No. 8 for the Yanks, from 1930 to 1943 and again in 1946. In a lineup that included Babe Ruth and Lou Gehrig, and later Gehrig and Joe DiMaggio, Dickey more than held his own, batting above .300 in eleven seasons. Dickey was a leader on the field, inspiring the Yankees with quiet hard work.

## ▲ MARTÍN DIHIGO
### Pitcher | NNL: 1923–1945

Dihigo is in the Hall as a pitcher for his long career in the Negro Leagues and Mexican League. His HOF plaque has him with more than 260 mound wins. He also led the Eastern Colored League twice in homers, and he regularly played shortstop in the winters in the Caribbean.

## JOE DIMAGGIO ▲

### Center Field | MLB: 1936–1951

In 1941, DiMaggio made history that no one has come close to topping. He had at least one hit in 56 games in a row. DiMaggio also helped the Yankees win nine World Series even though he missed three seasons fighting in World War II.

**IN OTHER WORDS**

"There is always some kid seeing me for the first time. I owe him my best."

**—Joe DiMaggio**

## ◀ LARRY DOBY

### Outfield | NNL: 1942–1947
### MLB: 1947–1959

While Jackie Robinson certainly deserves all the praise he gets, here's a big thumbs-up for Doby, the *second* Black player in the all-white majors. Doby joined Cleveland in July 1947, after Robinson made his debut that April. Doby went on to lead the AL in homers twice and was a seven-time AL All-Star.

## BOBBY DOERR ▶

**Second Base** | **MLB: 1937–1951**

Doerr did all the little things right and played his role perfectly. On an offensive powerhouse like the Ted Williams–led Red Sox of the 1940s and 1950s, Doerr was a nine-time All-Star in recognition of his solid defense and table-setting abilities.

## ◀ DON DRYSDALE

**Pitcher** | **MLB: 1956–1969**

Drysdale protected home plate ferociously. He was an old-school pitcher in the 1960s, a time of great change, but he still put together a record string of 58 2/3 scoreless innings in 1968. After his retirement in 1969, he became a popular broadcaster.

## HUGH DUFFY ▶

**Outfield** | **MLB: 1888–1901, 1904–1906**

No one has topped what Duffy did in 1894. His .440 average was the highest ever for a single season at the time. He was also a fine outfielder and later a hitting coach. One of his students? Ted Williams!

### ◀ DENNIS ECKERSLEY

**Pitcher** | **MLB: 1975–1998**

"Eck" was a solid starter for Boston and Oakland, but by 1987, he had become a reliever. He piled up 390 saves, including AL-bests twice, and his top season was in 1992, when he was the AL MVP and Cy Young Award winner.

## " IN OTHER WORDS "

Dennis Eckersley had a colorful way of speaking. He helped make slang like this a part of baseball:

- **Cheese or gas: a really fast fastball**
- **High cheese: a fastball up in the zone**
- **Punchout: a strikeout**
- **Salad: an off-speed or easy-to-hit pitch**

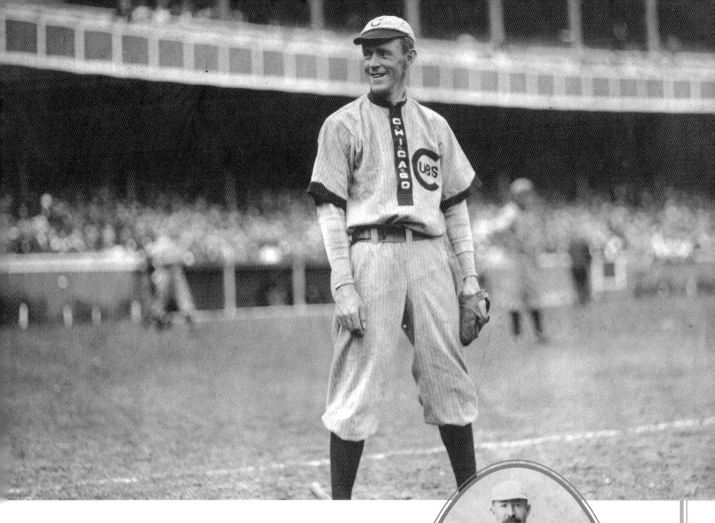

## JOHNNY EVERS ▲

**Second Base** | **MLB: 1902–1917, 1922, 1929**

Evers is famous for being part of a poem that talked
about the double-play combo for the Chicago Cubs.
He helped the Cubbies win the World Series in
1907 and 1908, and in 1914 he was part of the Boston
Braves' "miracle" season. The Braves came from
15 games back in July to win the Series.

## BUCK EWING ▶

**Catcher** | **MLB: 1880–1897**

Ewing played baseball's toughest position without any
protective gear! Few backstops lasted as long as he did in those
rough early days. Ewing set the standard for the position, and
he was one of the best overall hitters of the late 1800s, too.

## EXECUTIVES

**H**ere are a few people from the category of Hall of Famers that includes team owners, general managers, and pioneers of the early game, as well as people who had a big influence on the game in other ways.

**ED BARROW:** After managing the Red Sox to the 1918 World Series title (and moving a guy named Babe Ruth to the outfield), Barrow joined Ruth with the Yankees. As general manager, Barrow put together teams that won 14 AL pennants and 10 World Series titles.

**ALEXANDER CARTWRIGHT:** He played a key role in the Knickerbocker Baseball Club in New York City in the 1840s, helping establish early rules and taking part in the first games.

**HENRY CHADWICK:** Born in England, he became baseball's first national voice. Along with inventing the box score, Chadwick wrote about baseball for more than 40 years, playing a key role in making it nationally popular.

**CHARLES COMISKEY:** After playing and managing, Comiskey turned to team ownership with the Chicago White Sox. Along with others, he helped establish the American League in 1901.

**CANDY CUMMINGS:** This 1860s pitcher is given credit for inventing—or at least making popular—the curveball. Hitters have grumbled ever since!

**PAT GILLICK:** Gillick built the Toronto Blue Jays teams that won the 1992 and 1993 World Series. He also ran a 2008 Series winner in Philadelphia and was in charge of the Orioles and Mariners, too.

**BAN JOHNSON:** This former sportswriter led the drive to create the American League in 1901, and he was its president until 1927.

**EFFA MANLEY:** The only woman in the Hall of Fame, Manley co-owned the Newark Eagles of the Negro National League and played a big role in helping run that league.

**MARVIN MILLER:** He never played, but he had a big part in the sport. Miller led the Major League Baseball Players Association for 16 key years. During that time, he helped players gain free agent rights and earn bigger contracts than ever.

**WALTER O'MALLEY:** O'Malley spread baseball from coast to coast when he moved his Brooklyn Dodgers to Los Angeles in 1958. He built Dodger Stadium and saw his teams win three World Series before his son Peter took over in 1969.

**BUCK O'NEIL:** O'Neil had a long Negro Leagues career as a first baseman and manager. He was the first Black coach in the National League, joining the Cubs in 1962, and in his honor, the Hall of Fame gives an award for contributions to baseball.

**CUMBERLAND POSEY:** After playing for the NNL's Homestead Grays, he became the team owner in 1920. Under Posey, the Grays were a perennial superstar team until his death in 1946.

**BRANCH RICKEY:** Before signing Jackie Robinson in 1947, Rickey had already won three World Series with the Cardinals in the 1920s and 1930s as a legendary general manager. He took over the Dodgers in 1942 and built the team that won seven NL pennants and the 1955 World Series.

**ALBERT SPALDING:** This righty first gained fame as a star pitcher. After his career, he began a sporting goods company that made all the AL and NL baseballs. He helped spread baseball's popularity by making gear available to millions. He also published a popular baseball guide.

**BILL VEECK:** As an executive with the Cubs and an owner with Cleveland, the White Sox, and the Browns, Veeck delighted in making baseball fun as he invented many in-game promotions that are still used today. Veeck also signed Larry Doby in 1947 as the AL's first Black player.

**GEORGE AND HARRY WRIGHT:** These Wright brothers were nationally famous before the other Wright brothers invented the airplane. George Wright was a star shortstop for the Cincinnati Red Stockings of 1869. Harry Wright was the team manager and guided Boston into the National Association, the first major league, in 1871.

## BOB FELLER ▲
### Pitcher | MLB: 1936–1956

By the time he was 19, Feller was leading the AL in strikeouts for the first of seven times, and when he was 20, he led in wins for the first of six seasons. He gave up three years of his baseball career to fight in World War II but came back just as fast as before.

## ◀ ROLLIE FINGERS
### Pitcher | MLB: 1968–1985

Fingers led his league three times in saves with a career total of 341. He was a key part of Oakland's World Series wins from 1972 to 1974. He had his best season in 1981, when he won the AL Cy Young and the MVP with the Milwaukee Brewers.

## CARLTON FISK ▶

### Catcher | MLB: 1969–1993

Tall for a catcher at 6'3", Fisk was a key leader for the Red Sox and White Sox. After winning AL Rookie of the Year in 1972, he helped Boston reach the 1975 World Series. His 12th-inning homer won Game 6—after he "helped" it stay fair with some famous arm-waving!

**MAGIC MOMENT**

**October 21, 1975:** Carlton Fisk frantically waved his arms, pleading with the baseball to stay in fair territory. Fisk's wish was granted when his twefth-inning home run in Game 6 of the 1975 World Series bounced off the left field foul pole at Fenway Park, giving his Boston Red Sox a 7-6 win and sending the Fall Classic to Game 7.

6'3"

# ◀ EDWARD "WHITEY" FORD

## Pitcher | MLB: 1950–1967

On great Yankees' teams in the 1950s
and 1960s, Ford was the star pitcher. No
one has won more World Series games
than Ford's 10. He also led the AL three
times in wins, was a 10-time All-Star,
and won the 1961 AL Cy Young Award.

## ◀ JIMMIE FOXX

**First Base** | **MLB: 1925–1945**

"Double X" was one of baseball's greatest sluggers. Foxx hit more homers in the 1930s than any other player, and he led the AL four times, with a high of 58 in 1932, on the way to a career total of 534. He also won the 1933 Triple Crown and was a three-time AL MVP.

## ◀ FRANKIE FRISCH

**Second Base** | **MLB: 1919–1937**

Frisch was one of the top players of the first half of the 1900s. He had a career .316 average, led the NL in steals three times, and was probably the top-fielding second sacker of the time. He won four World Series, two with the Giants and two with the Cardinals.

## PUD GALVIN ▶

### Pitcher | MLB: 1875-1892

In the 1800s, "Pud" pitched often, he completed games, and he won . . . over and over. Galvin still holds three career records: most complete games, losses, and hits in one league. His endurance was probably most impressive: In 1883 he started 75 games, finished 72, and won 46 of them.

OLD JUDGE CIGARETTES Goodwin & Co., New York.

## ◀ LOU GEHRIG

### First Base | MLB: 1923-1939

Gehrig is one of baseball's most beloved stars. He helped the Yankees win seven World Series, but had to end his career because of ALS, a nerve disease. He had seven seasons with 150 RBI, and he also led the league in RBI five times, with a career high of 185 in 1931.

**MAGIC MOMENT**

**July 4, 1939: Lou Gehrig is honored at Yankee Stadium after he has to retire due to the disease that would later be named for him. He gives a speech calling himself "the luckiest man on the face of the Earth." He died less than two years later.**

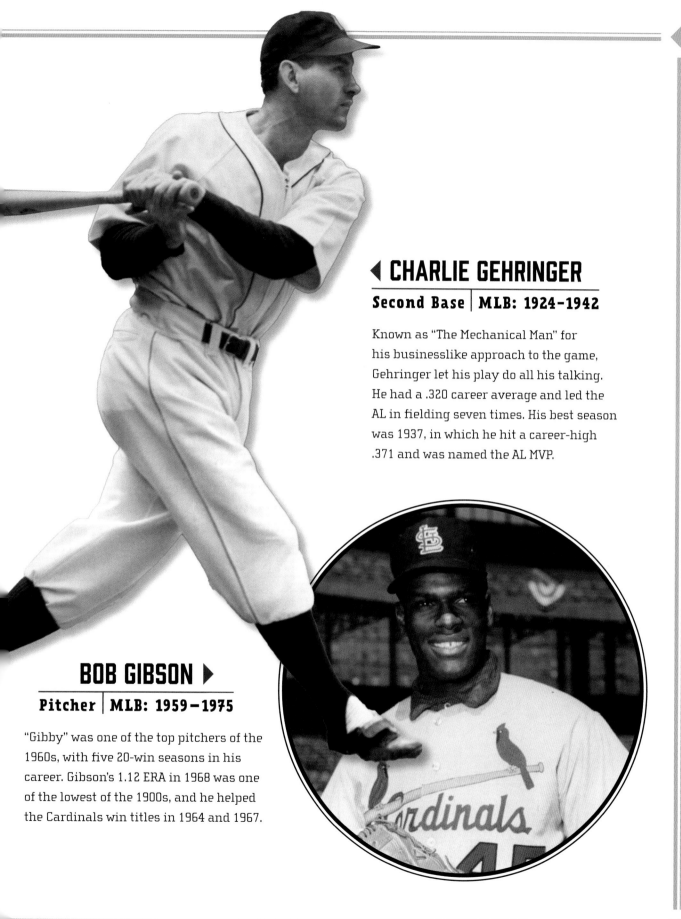

## ◀ CHARLIE GEHRINGER

### Second Base | MLB: 1924–1942

Known as "The Mechanical Man" for his businesslike approach to the game, Gehringer let his play do all his talking. He had a .320 career average and led the AL in fielding seven times. His best season was 1937, in which he hit a career-high .371 and was named the AL MVP.

## BOB GIBSON ▶

### Pitcher | MLB: 1959–1975

"Gibby" was one of the top pitchers of the 1960s, with five 20-win seasons in his career. Gibson's 1.12 ERA in 1968 was one of the lowest of the 1900s, and he helped the Cardinals win titles in 1964 and 1967.

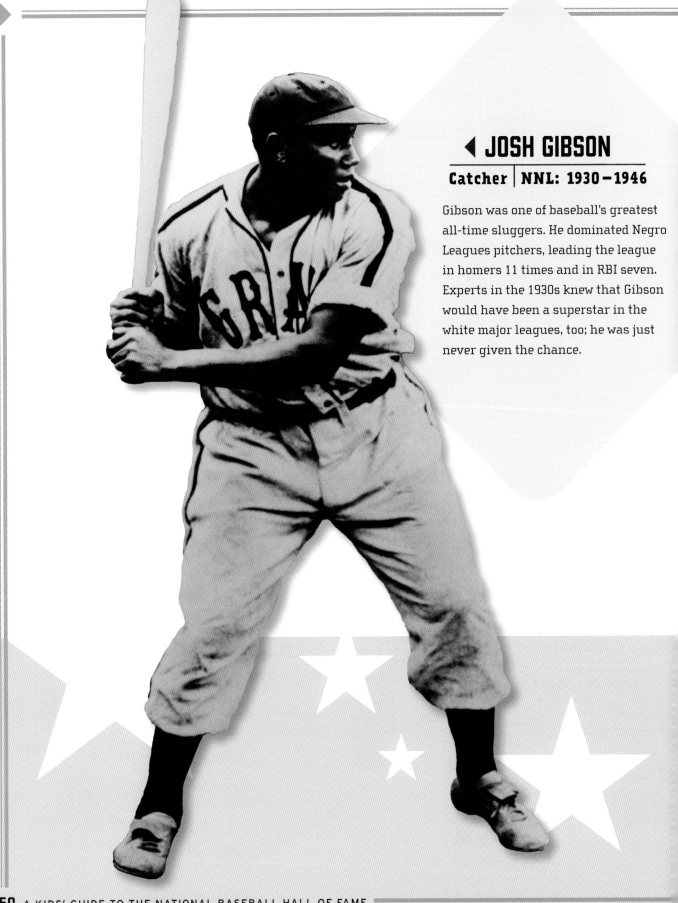

## ◀ JOSH GIBSON

### Catcher | NNL: 1930–1946

Gibson was one of baseball's greatest all-time sluggers. He dominated Negro Leagues pitchers, leading the league in homers 11 times and in RBI seven. Experts in the 1930s knew that Gibson would have been a superstar in the white major leagues, too; he was just never given the chance.

## TOM GLAVINE ▶

**Pitcher** | **MLB: 1987–2008**

Glavine played in the major leagues for 22 seasons, earning ten All-Star bids and a pair of Cy Young Awards along the way. He was a key part of the great Braves pitching staff that helped Atlanta win 14 straight NL East titles and, in 1995, a World Series. Glavine was named the Series MVP. He later earned his 300th career win with the Mets in 2007 at the age of 41.

## ◀ LEFTY GOMEZ

**Pitcher** | **MLB: 1930–1943**

The Yankees dominated baseball in the 1930s, and Gomez was a big reason. While his teammates Ruth, Gehrig, and DiMaggio were smacking the ball, Gomez was putting up zeroes. In five World Series, he was 6-0 with a 2.86 ERA.

## ◀ GOOSE GOSLIN
### Left Field | MLB: 1921–1938

Leon "Goose" Goslin once said of the game he loved, "It was more than fun. It was heaven." But it wasn't all play and no work! He topped 100 RBI 11 times, among the most ever, and topped .315 eight times, while helping both the Senators and Tigers win World Series championships.

## GOOSE GOSSAGE ▶
### Relief Pitcher | MLB: 1972–1994

Another "Goose" in the Hall of Fame found his way there in 2008. Relief pitcher Gossage was a three-time AL saves leader, with a powerful fastball and a style that just about dared opponents to beat him . . . at their peril.

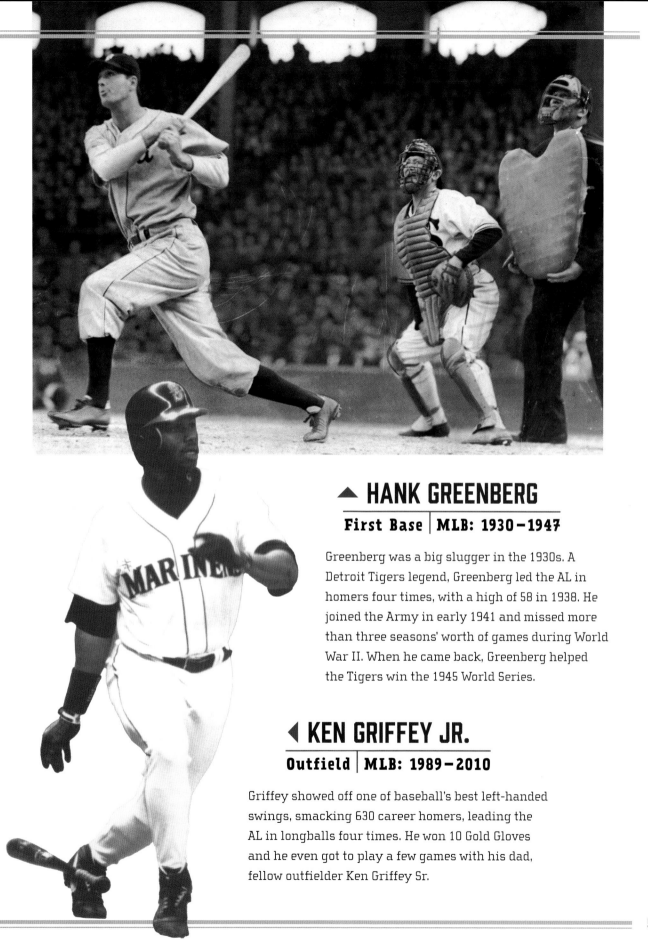

## ▲ HANK GREENBERG
### First Base | MLB: 1930–1947

Greenberg was a big slugger in the 1930s. A
Detroit Tigers legend, Greenberg led the AL in
homers four times, with a high of 58 in 1938. He
joined the Army in early 1941 and missed more
than three seasons' worth of games during World
War II. When he came back, Greenberg helped
the Tigers win the 1945 World Series.

## ◄ KEN GRIFFEY JR.
### Outfield | MLB: 1989–2010

Griffey showed off one of baseball's best left-handed
swings, smacking 630 career homers, leading the
AL in longballs four times. He won 10 Gold Gloves
and he even got to play a few games with his dad,
fellow outfielder Ken Griffey Sr.

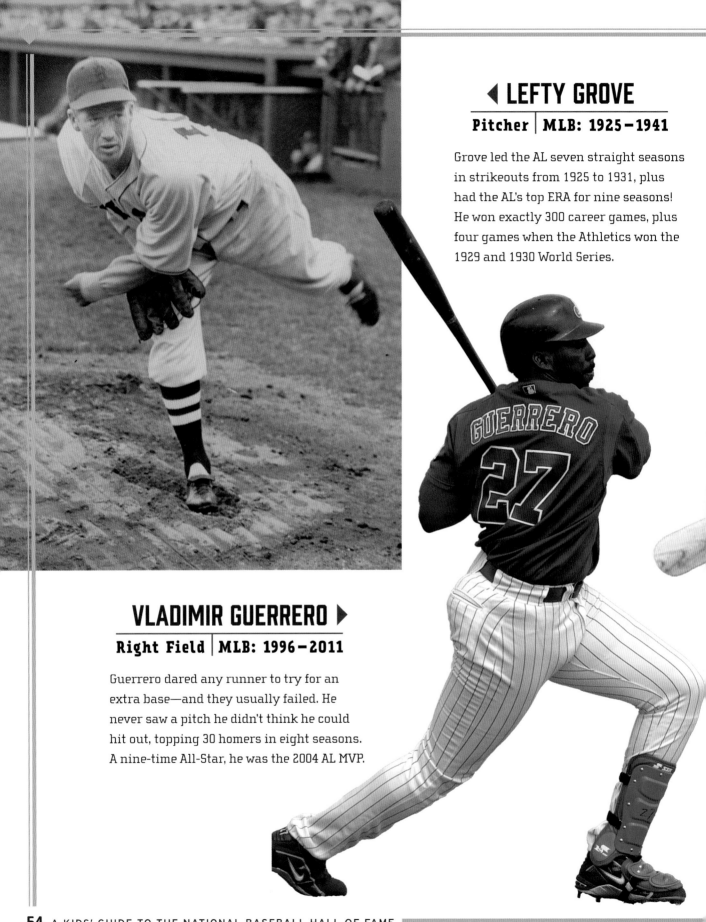

## ◀ LEFTY GROVE

### Pitcher | MLB: 1925–1941

Grove led the AL seven straight seasons in strikeouts from 1925 to 1931, plus had the AL's top ERA for nine seasons! He won exactly 300 career games, plus four games when the Athletics won the 1929 and 1930 World Series.

## VLADIMIR GUERRERO ▶

### Right Field | MLB: 1996–2011

Guerrero dared any runner to try for an extra base—and they usually failed. He never saw a pitch he didn't think he could hit out, topping 30 homers in eight seasons. A nine-time All-Star, he was the 2004 AL MVP.

## TONY GWYNN ▶
### Right Field | MLB: 1982–2001

No one has more National League batting titles than Gwynn's eight, and he also led the NL in hits seven times. His 1994 mark of .394 is the highest for a single season since the 1940s. Gwynn was a 15-time All-Star and a five-time Gold Glove winner.

## ROY HALLADAY ▲

### Pitcher | MLB: 1998–2013

Halladay is one of only six pitchers to earn a Cy Young Award in both the AL and the NL. He won with Toronto in 2003, when he led the AL in wins. In 2010 with Philadelphia, he threw a perfect game and later had the second no-hitter in postseason history in an NLDS game.

## BILLY HAMILTON ▶

### Outfield | MLB: 1888–1901

"Sliding" Billy Hamilton set the standards for base-stealers. He used his great speed to lead his league in thefts five times. Four times he had 100 or more steals in a season.

HAMILTON L.F. KANSAS CITY.

OLD JUDGE CIGARETTES Goodwin & Co., New York.

## ◀ GABBY HARTNETT

### Catcher | MLB: 1922–1941

Hartnett became the first catcher in baseball history to reach 1,000 RBI and 200 homers, all with a .297 career batting average. He also led NL catchers in fielding percentage and assists six times each. As the 1935 NL MVP, Hartnett is well remembered for hitting the "Homer in the Gloamin'," giving the Cubs a late-inning win in 1938.

## TODD HELTON ▶

### First Base | MLB: 1997–2013

Helton was one of the top sluggers of the early 2000s. Some say he took advantage of hitting in the thin, mile-high air of Denver's Coors Field. But this 17-season Rockie could rock no matter where he played. He was an NL batting champ and had a career .316 batting average.

## ◀ RICKEY HENDERSON

### Outfield | MLB: 1979-2003

Henderson's 2,295 runs scored are the most in history. At the same time, he was also the best base-stealer of all time, with 1,406—almost 500 more than Lou Brock in second place. His electric speed and solid bat made him a 10-time All-Star and the 1990 AL MVP.

**MAGIC MOMENT**

**May 1, 1991:** Rickey Henderson grabbed third base and thrust both his arms in the air, celebrating his 939th career stolen base. The successful steal of third for the A's superstar broke Lou Brock's all-time record.

## GIL HODGES

**First Base | MLB: 1943–1963**

Hodges was one of the offensive forces on the Brooklyn Dodgers' great 1950s teams. He had at least 100 RBI in seven straight seasons, and he was part of the Dodgers' famous 1955 World Series win. After the team moved to LA, he helped win the Series again in 1959.

## ◀ TREVOR HOFFMAN

**Pitcher | MLB: 1993–2010**

Hoffman racked up 601 saves as one of the top closers of all time. He led the NL twice, and had 40 or more saves nine times. Today, the top reliever in the NL each season receives the Trevor Hoffman Award.

## ◀ ROGERS HORNSBY

### Second Base | MLB: 1915–1937

Hornsby averaged .397 from 1920 to 1925, when he won six of his seven NL batting titles. His .358 career average is third all-time almost 100 years after his final game. He could do it all, leading the NL in runs, hits, RBI, and homers.

## CARL HUBBELL ▶

### Pitcher | MLB: 1928–1943

Hubbell was a three-time NL wins leader and also three times an ERA champ. He was a steady winner for the New York Giants and helped them win the 1933 World Series.

July 10, 1934: Carl Hubbell strikes out five future Hall of Famers in a row at the 1934 All-Star Game: Babe Ruth, Lou Gehrig, Jimmie Foxx, Al Simmons, and Joe Cronin. Look for all of their names in this book!

### ◀ CATFISH HUNTER

**Pitcher | MLB: 1965–1979**

Hunter helped the A's win three World Series (1972, 1973, and 1974). He threw a perfect game in 1968 and later earned the 1974 AL Cy Young Award. He moved to the Yankees in 1975, led the AL in wins, and then helped New York win two more Series, in 1977 and 1978.

## ▼ MONTE IRVIN

**Outfield** | **NNL: 1938–1948**
**MLB: 1949–1956**

Irvin played six full Negro League seasons before his eight NL seasons. He was a league-leading hitter with the Newark Eagles, then moved to the New York Giants in 1949. He led the NL with 121 RBI in 1951 and won World Series titles with Newark in 1946 and the Giants in 1954.

# INTERNATIONAL All-Stars

**B**aseball has become a truly international game. The International Baseball Federation has more than 125 nations as members. Members of the Hall of Fame (through 2024) have been born in nine countries or territories outside the United States. Those birthplaces are listed with the number of Hall of Famers born there.

- *Cuba* (6)
- *Puerto Rico* (4)
- *Dominican Republic* (5)
- *England* (3)
- *Canada* (2)
- *Panama* (2)
- *Venezuela* (1)
- *Netherlands* (1)
- *Germany* (1)

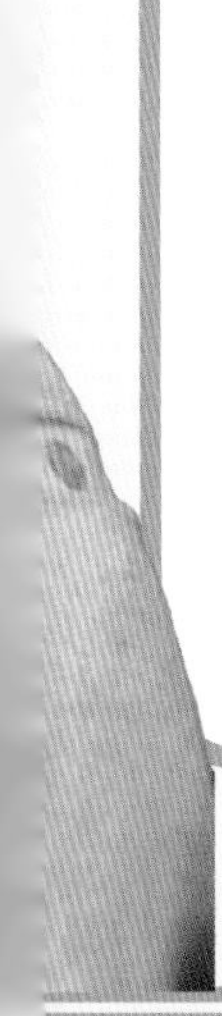

## MAGIC MOMENT

**October 18, 1977:** As the baseball sailed over Yankee Stadium's center field fence and into the night, Reggie Jackson officially became Mr. October. Reggie's third home run in Game 6 of the 1977 World Series clinched his Fall Classic MVP Award and helped the Bronx Bombers win their 22nd championship.

## ◀ REGGIE JACKSON

### Right Field | MLB: 1967–1987

With Oakland, Jackson was the MVP of the 1973 World Series and also helped them win again in 1972 and 1974. He got his second Series MVP in 1977 with the Yankees. Nicknamed "Mr. October," Jackson had 10 homers and 24 RBI in 27 World Series games.

# FERGIE JENKINS ▶

## Pitcher | MLB: 1965–1983

Jenkins was a dependable winning pitcher for three teams, reaching 20 wins in seven seasons. He led the AL and NL once each in Ws. His best season was 1971, when he won 24 games for the Cubs and earned the Cy Young Award.

## ◄ DEREK JETER

### Shortstop | MLB: 1995–2014

For almost 20 seasons, Yankees fans knew that "The Captain" would be there for them. Jeter recorded fewer than 600 plate appearances just once from 1996 to 2012. A career .310 hitter, he finished with 3,465 hits, sixth all-time. He was a key part of five World Series winners, earning MVP honors in 2000.

**MOMENT**

September 25, 2014: Near the end of his Hall of Fame career, Derek Jeter comes through for the Yankees one more time. His last at-bat in Yankee Stadium is a game-winning, walk-off single to right field.

## JUDY JOHNSON ▶
### Third Base | NNL: 1923–1936

Johnson was the first third baseman elected from the Negro Leagues, both a solid hitter and an outstanding defensive player. He helped Hilldale and Pittsburgh win World Series titles. Johnson topped .300 in five seasons and was tops in hits twice.

## ◀ RANDY JOHNSON
### Pitcher | MLB: 1988–2009

Johnson was one of baseball's most dominant pitchers. He was a nine-time league strikeout king and a four-time ERA champ. Johnson's most memorable season came in 2001, when he was the World Series co-MVP for Arizona after winning two games and then coming in late to win Game 7 to clinch it! His five Cy Young Awards are second-most all-time.

## BIG
### NUMBER

## 24
The number of perfect games thrown in baseball history, through 2023. Seven were thrown by Hall of Famers: Randy Johnson, John Ward, Cy Young, Addie Joss, Sandy Koufax, Catfish Hunter, and Roy Halladay.

## WALTER JOHNSON ▶
### Pitcher | MLB: 1907–1927

Johnson dominated AL hitters for years, leading the league in wins six times, ERA five times, and strikeouts 12 times (including eight in a row!). His 110 shutouts are the most ever, and his 417 career wins are second only to Cy Young.

## ◀ CHIPPER JONES

### Third Base | MLB: 1993–2012

Jones's bat and glove were a big part of the Atlanta Braves' run of 11 NL East Division titles in a row from 1995 to 2005. He also helped them win the 1995 World Series and earned the 1999 NL MVP Award.

## ADDIE JOSS ▶

### Pitcher | MLB: 1902–1910

Second all-time with a 1.89 career ERA, Joss had a great career cut short when he died at only 30 years old. He was a two-time AL ERA champ and won 20 games in four seasons. His career highlight came in 1908, when he threw the fourth perfect game ever.

# K

## JIM KAAT ▶

### Pitcher | MLB: 1959–1983

The man they called "Kitty" prowled Major League mounds for 25 years on five teams. Kaat helped the Twins reach the 1965 World Series with 18 wins, then put up a career-best 25 victories the following season. Kaat also excelled as a fielder, winning a then-record 16 Gold Glove Awards at his position. He capped off his career with a World Series win with the Cardinals in 1982 at the age of 43.

## ◀ AL KALINE

### Outfield | MLB: 1953–1974

Kaline was a Tiger through and through for 22 seasons. He was an 18-time All-Star and won 10 Gold Gloves for his great defense in the outfield. He helped the Tigers win the 1968 World Series title and he's also part of the 3,000-hit club.

## TIM KEEFE ▶

### Pitcher | MLB: 1880–1893

Keefe was one of the dominant pitchers of baseball's early decades. He was a league leader at various times in wins, ERA, complete games, and strikeouts. His best season might have been 1888, when he won 19 games in a row on the way to a league-best 35 Ws and a 1.74 ERA.

OLD JUDGE CIGARETTES Goodwin & Co., New York.

## ◀ WILLIE KEELER
### Right Field | MLB: 1892–1910

You can still follow Willie Keeler's great advice today: "Hit 'em where they ain't." In his 19 seasons, he put together a .341 lifetime average and an NL-record 44-game hitting streak. His record of eight straight seasons with at least 200 hits was not passed until 2009 by Ichiro Suzuki.

## KING KELLY ▶
### Outfield | MLB: 1878–1893

Kelly was one of the most popular and inventive players of the late 1800s. In a time when baseball was still growing, Kelly helped create familiar plays like the double steal, the hit-and-run, and shifting outfielders.

**IN OTHER WORDS**

**Double steal:** When two teammates steal a base at the same time.

**Hit-and-run:** A play in which a baserunner takes off before the batter hits the ball into play.

# HARMON KILLEBREW

**First Base** | **MLB: 1954–1975**

Killebrew didn't become a regular for his team until his sixth season, but he made the most of his chance when it came, leading the AL in homers for the first of six times. Killebrew topped 40 homers in eight seasons. He was a 13-time All-Star and the 1969 AL MVP.

## RALPH KINER ▶

### Left Field | MLB: 1946–1955

A back problem limited Kiner to only 10 seasons, but he made the most of them. While with the Pittsburgh Pirates, he led the NL in homers in each of the first seven seasons of his career, something no other player has done. At home in "Kiner's Korner," he was later a beloved longtime broadcaster with the New York Mets.

## CHUCK KLEIN ▼

### Right Field | MLB: 1928–1944

Klein led the NL at least once each in runs, hits, doubles, homers, RBI, steals, slugging percentage, and batting average. His best season came in 1933, when he won the Triple Crown.

## BIG NUMBER

### 16

The number of different Hall of Famers who have won a batting Triple Crown (leading a league in batting average, HR, and RBI in the same season). Oscar Charleston (NNL) is the only player to win three, while Josh Gibson (NNL), Rogers Hornsby (NL), and Ted Williams (AL) won two each.

## SANDY KOUFAX ▲

### Pitcher | MLB: 1955–1966

From 1961 to 1966, Koufax may have been
the best pitcher of all time. In those years,
he won five straight NL ERA titles, three Cy
Young Awards, the 1963 NL MVP, and four
strikeout titles. He also had four no-hitters,
including a perfect game in 1965. Plus
he helped the Dodgers win four
World Series titles.

## NAP LAJOIE ▶

### Second Base | MLB: 1896–1916

Lajoie was a five-time AL batting and three-time RBI champ with 3,243 career hits. His 1901 season was one of the best ever, when he won the Triple Crown, and his .426 average was the highest in MLB in the 1900s. Lajoie was part of the second class in Hall of Fame history in 1937.

## ◀ BARRY LARKIN

### Shortstop | MLB: 1986–2004

A 12-time All-Star, Larkin helped Cincinnati win the 1990 World Series and was later the 1995 NL MVP. His speed helped make him the first shortstop with 30 homers and 30 steals in a season (1996).

### ◀ BOB LEMON

**Pitcher** | **MLB: 1946–1958**

Bob Lemon is a perfect example of the old saying, "If at first you don't succeed, try, try again." He struggled so much for the Indians that he was almost moved to the outfield, but he made the most of his chance. By 1948, he was a regular in the All-Star Game and a 20-game winner, and he went on to help the then-Cleveland Indians reach the World Series twice.

### WALTER "BUCK" LEONARD ▶

**First Base** | **NNL: 1935–1948**

Leonard was part of the dominant Homestead Grays lineup for 14 seasons, leading the league in homers, average, slugging, and on-base percentage at least once each. And he helped the Grays win a pair of Negro League World Series titles.

## JOHN HENRY "POP" LLOYD ▶

**Shortstop** | **NNL: 1921–1929**

Lloyd was a superstar in the Cuban leagues, as well as one of the top hitters on teams that played before the Negro Leagues were organized in 1920. As a hitter, he was a great bunter, and on defense, you had to hit the ball pretty hard to get it past him.

# M

## GREG MADDUX ▶

### Pitcher | MLB: 1986–2008

With 355 wins (eighth all-time), four Cy Young Awards, and an all-time record 18 Gold Gloves, Maddux is one of the top pitchers of the past 100 years. He won his fourth straight Cy Young Award in 1995, the year he helped the Atlanta Braves win the World Series.

### ◀ MICKEY MANTLE

**Center Field | MLB: 1951–1968**

Mantle was one of baseball's great all-around superstars, leading the AL in homers four times on his way to 536 career homers. "The Mick" won three AL MVP awards and was part of 12 AL championship teams and seven World Series winners.

## BIG NUMBER

### 18

**The number of career World Series homers hit by Mickey Mantle, still the all-time record.**

### JUAN MARICHAL ▶

**Pitcher | MLB: 1960–1975**

Marichal had an overpowering fastball, but great control. His career WHIP (walks plus hits per innings pitched) mark was a super-low 1.101. A native of the Dominican Republic, Marichal had six 20-win seasons in the 1960s, leading the league in 1963 and 1968.

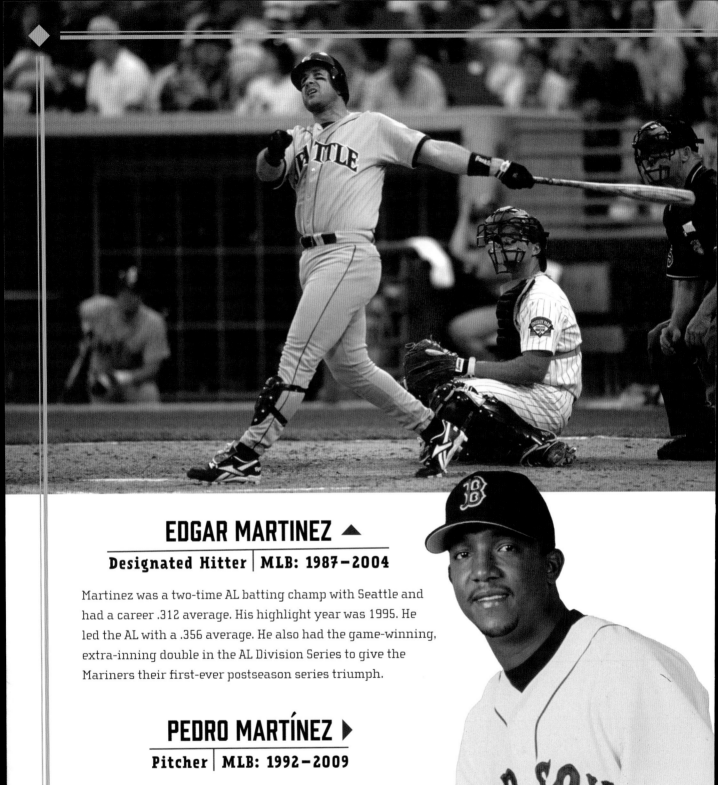

## EDGAR MARTINEZ ▲

### Designated Hitter | MLB: 1987–2004

Martinez was a two-time AL batting champ with Seattle and had a career .312 average. His highlight year was 1995. He led the AL with a .356 average. He also had the game-winning, extra-inning double in the AL Division Series to give the Mariners their first-ever postseason series triumph.

## PEDRO MARTÍNEZ ▶

### Pitcher | MLB: 1992–2009

From 1993 to 2007, Martínez never lost more than 10 games in a season. Martínez earned three Cy Young Awards, one with Montreal and two more with Boston. He was at his finest with the Red Sox, helping them win the 2004 World Series.

## ◀ EDDIE MATHEWS
### Third Base | MLB: 1952–1968

What athlete was featured on the first issue of *Sports Illustrated* in 1954? You're reading about him! From 1952 to 1959, no one hit more homers than Eddie Mathews. He ended up with 512 homers for his career, then the most by a third baseman. He's also the only player to play with the Braves franchise in all three of its homes: Boston, Milwaukee, and Atlanta.

## CHRISTY MATHEWSON ▶
### Pitcher | MLB: 1900–1916

Mathewson led the NL in wins four times and in ERA in five seasons. His 373 wins are tied for third-most all-time, while his 2.13 ERA is still ninth best. No pitcher will ever repeat his greatest triumph: three complete-game shutouts in six days to lead the New York Giants to the 1905 World Series crown.

## ◀ JOE MAUER

**Catcher | MLB: 2004–2018**

Catchers have a hard enough job playing their
position. Catchers who can hit well are pretty rare.
Mauer is even more rare—he is the only catcher to
win three batting titles in the AL. He grew up in
Minnesota and played his whole career with
the Twins. He was the 2009 AL MVP and
had a career .306 average.

## WILLIE MAYS ▶

**Center Field | NNL: 1948; MLB: 1951–1973**

On the very, very short list of greatest all-around
players, the "Say Hey Kid" has a permanent spot.
Mays hit 660 homers, earned four NL stolen-base
crowns, and won a record-tying 12 outfield
Gold Gloves. A two-time NL MVP, he was in
24 All-Star Games and helped the Giants
to a 1954 World Series win.

**MAGIC MOMENT**

September 29, 1954: Willie Mays makes one of the
most memorable catches in baseball history. In Game 1
of the World Series, he races back on a long ball hit by
Cleveland's Vic Wertz. Mays makes "The Catch" with his
back to home plate and the fans went wild.

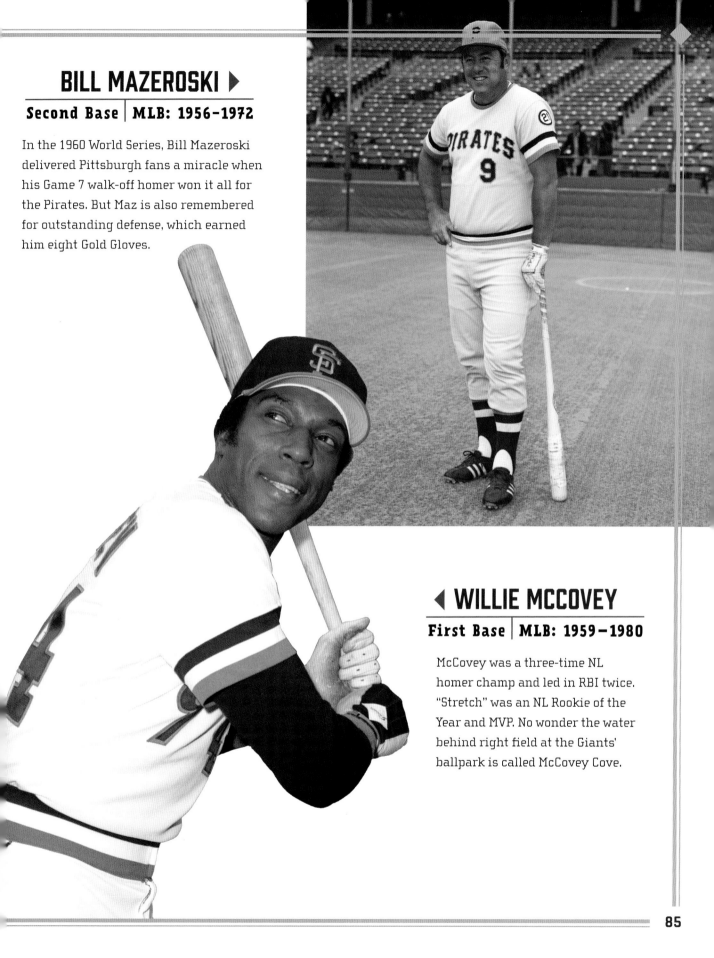

# BILL MAZEROSKI ▶

**Second Base | MLB: 1956–1972**

In the 1960 World Series, Bill Mazeroski delivered Pittsburgh fans a miracle when his Game 7 walk-off homer won it all for the Pirates. But Maz is also remembered for outstanding defense, which earned him eight Gold Gloves.

# ◀ WILLIE MCCOVEY

**First Base | MLB: 1959–1980**

McCovey was a three-time NL homer champ and led in RBI twice. "Stretch" was an NL Rookie of the Year and MVP. No wonder the water behind right field at the Giants' ballpark is called McCovey Cove.

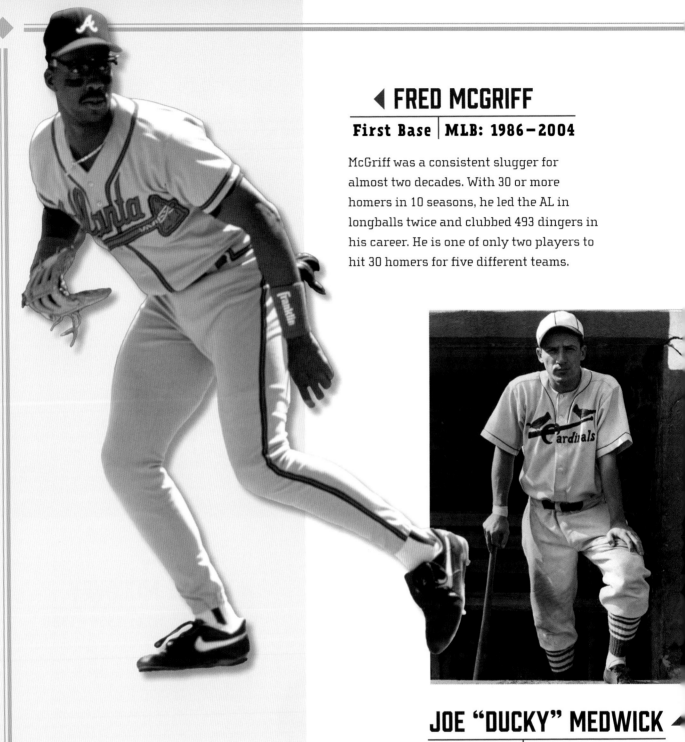

## ◀ FRED MCGRIFF

### First Base | MLB: 1986–2004

McGriff was a consistent slugger for
almost two decades. With 30 or more
homers in 10 seasons, he led the AL in
longballs twice and clubbed 493 dingers in
his career. He is one of only two players to
hit 30 homers for five different teams.

## JOE "DUCKY" MEDWICK ◀

### Left Field | MLB: 1932–1948

Medwick earned the Triple Crown title
and the NL MVP in 1937, plus one of his
10 career All-Star selections. In 1934,
Medwick hit .379 in the World Series to
help the Cardinals win the ring.

## ◀ MINNIE MIÑOSO

**Outfield** | **NNL: 1946–1948**
**MLB: 1949–1964, 1976, 1980**

Miñoso was a pioneer, the first big AL/NL star to come from Latin America. His speed and great defense made him a seven-time All-Star in the AL and three-time stolen-base king. Miñoso also excelled at being hit by pitches, leading the majors 10 painful times!

## PAUL MOLITOR ▶

**Third Base** | **MLB: 1978–1998**

Molitor piled up a .306 career average and is one of only seven players with over 3,000 hits (3,319) and 500 (504) stolen bases. After 15 years with the Brewers, Molitor helped the Blue Jays win the 1993 World Series—and he was the Series MVP.

## ◀ JOE MORGAN

### Second Base | MLB: 1963–1984

By the time Morgan arrived in Cincinnati, he was already a nine-year veteran, but he became a sparkplug for the two-time World Series champs (1975 and 1976). He was also a two-time NL MVP. When he retired, his 268 homers were the most by a second baseman.

## EDDIE MURRAY ▶

### First Base | MLB: 1977–1997

Murray was a steady slugger and one of the best switch-hitters ever. He topped 25 homers in a season 12 times on his way to 504 in his career. In 1983, he helped the Orioles win the World Series.

## STAN MUSIAL ▶

### Outfield | MLB: 1941–1963

Musial led the NL at least once in runs, hits, doubles, triples, walks, and RBI. He was a three-time NL MVP in the 1940s and helped the Cardinals win three World Series. One of the great all-around stars, Musial's 3,630 hits are fourth-most all-time.

## ◀ MIKE MUSSINA

### Pitcher | MLB: 1991–2008

In 17 full seasons as a starter, Mussina had only one losing season. He pitched for the Orioles for 10 seasons and won 147 games, yet only made six postseason starts. When he joined the Yankees in 2001, he got a chance to shine in the playoffs and made 15 starts in 12 postseason series. In his last season, Mussina won a career-best 20 games to wrap up a 270-win career.

OFFICIAL LINE-UP

DATE:
TIME:
FIELD:

TEAM: HOME ☐ VISITOR ☐
OPPONENT:

# | STARTING PLAYER | POS | SUBSTITUTION
1
2
3
4
5
6
7
8
9
10
11
12
13
14
15
16

COACH: ____ UMPIRE COPY

# MANAGERS

The person in charge of a baseball team on the field is called the manager. As with players, some rise above the others to earn a spot in the Hall of Fame. Here are a few highlights from the 23 managers elected through 2024.

**TONY LA RUSSA:** This longtime baseball man is second all-time with 2,884 wins. La Russa won six league pennants and three World Series—one with the Athletics (1989) and two with the Cardinals (2006 and 2011).

**TOMMY LASORDA:** Known for his love of "Dodger Blue," Lasorda led the LA Dodgers to four NL pennants and two World Series wins (1981 and 1988).

**JIM LEYLAND:** A player's manager and three-time Manager of the Year, Leyland led both the Detroit Tigers and Florida Marlins to league pennants, capped by the Marlins' first World Series title in 1997. And that came after leading the Pittsburgh Pirates for 11 seasons and helping rebuild that club.

**CONNIE MACK:** The all-time leader in wins by a manager with 3,731, Mack led the Philadelphia Athletics as manager for 50 seasons (and owned the team for most of that time). Mack's A's won nine AL pennants and five World Series.

**JOHN MCGRAW:** This creative former player (Baltimore Orioles in the 1890s) became the fiery leader of New York Giants for 31 seasons, winning 10 NL pennants and three World Series.

**CASEY STENGEL:** Stengel was one of baseball's most famous "characters." Funny and beloved by fans for his witty sayings, the former outfielder led the New York Yankees to 10 AL pennants and seven World Series titles, and he was later the first manager of the New York Mets.

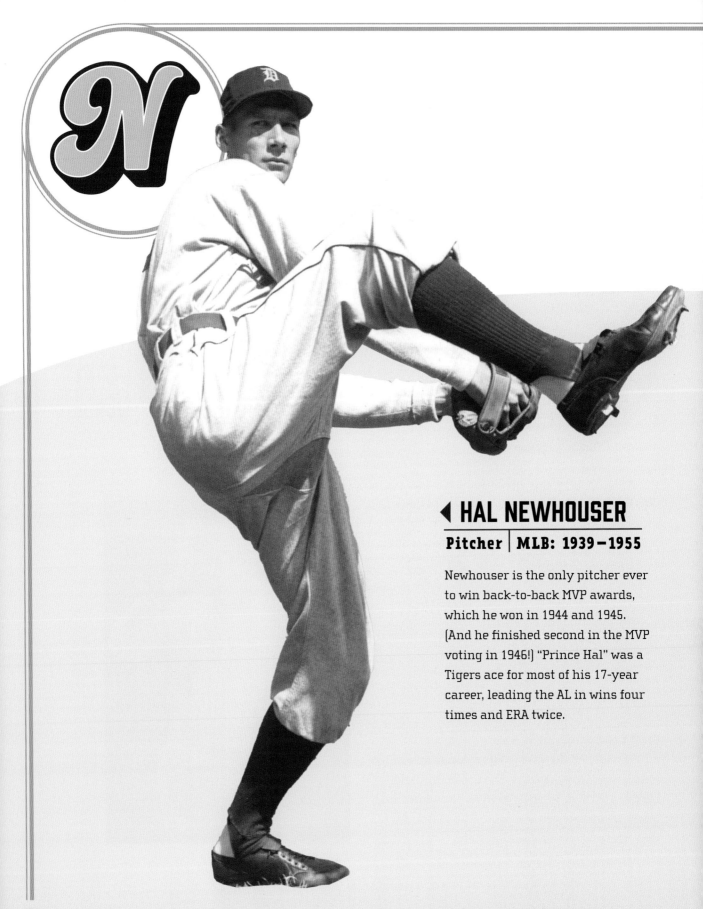

## ◄ HAL NEWHOUSER

### Pitcher | MLB: 1939–1955

Newhouser is the only pitcher ever to win back-to-back MVP awards, which he won in 1944 and 1945. (And he finished second in the MVP voting in 1946!) "Prince Hal" was a Tigers ace for most of his 17-year career, leading the AL in wins four times and ERA twice.

## PHIL NIEKRO ▶

**Pitcher** | **MLB: 1964–1987**

Niekro threw a pitch not often seen anymore: a knuckleball. The ball does not spin much and can often move in strange ways on its trip to the plate, but Niekro's knucklers found the strike zone often, helping him pile up 318 wins in his 24-year career.

## ◀ TONY OLIVA

**Right Field** | **MLB: 1962–197**

Oliva was the 1964 AL Rookie of the Yea with the Twins, and he was the first player ever to win a batting title in his first two full seasons. He led the AL in hits five times and doubles four times piling up a career .304 average.

## DAVID ORTIZ ▲
### Designated Hitter
### MLB: 1997–2016

Nicknamed "Big Papi," Ortiz was clutch in delivering walk-off hits and homers that thrilled Red Sox fans. He led Boston to three World Series titles, including the one in 2004 that broke an 86-year streak without a championship. He also led the AL with 127 RBI in his final season in 2016.

## ◄ MEL OTT
### Right Field | MLB: 1926–1947

With the New York Giants, Ott led the NL in homers six times in the 1930s and 1940s. The 12-time All-Star ended up with 511 homers. Ott also led the Giants to the 1933 World Series title and later to two more NL pennants.

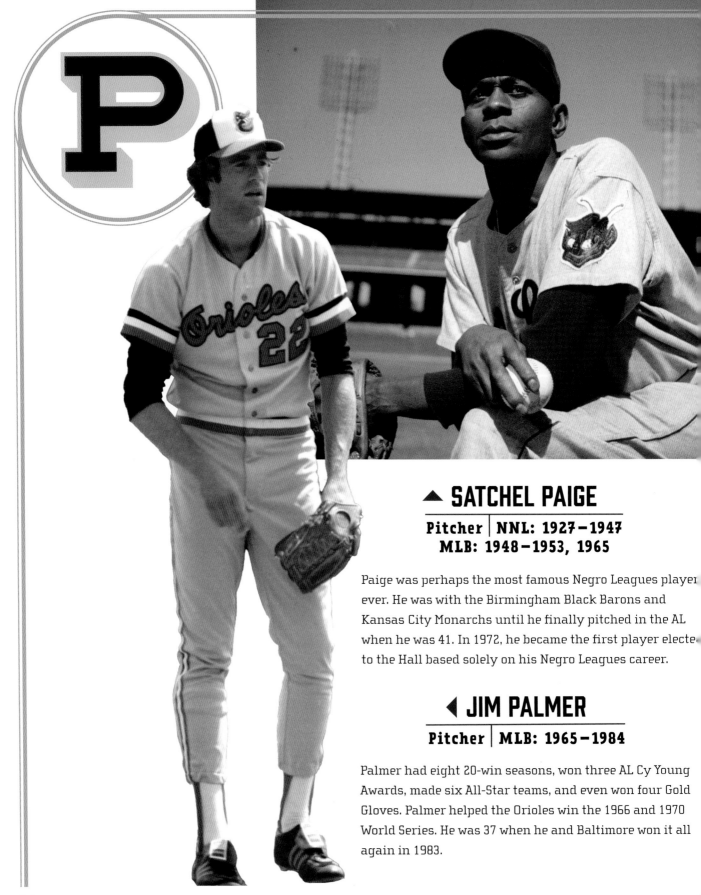

## ▲ SATCHEL PAIGE

**Pitcher** | **NNL: 1927–1947**
**MLB: 1948–1953, 1965**

Paige was perhaps the most famous Negro Leagues player ever. He was with the Birmingham Black Barons and Kansas City Monarchs until he finally pitched in the AL when he was 41. In 1972, he became the first player elected to the Hall based solely on his Negro Leagues career.

## ◀ JIM PALMER

**Pitcher** | **MLB: 1965–1984**

Palmer had eight 20-win seasons, won three AL Cy Young Awards, made six All-Star teams, and even won four Gold Gloves. Palmer helped the Orioles win the 1966 and 1970 World Series. He was 37 when he and Baltimore won it all again in 1983.

## MIKE PIAZZA ▶

### Catcher | MLB: 1992–2007

Piazza was not picked until the 62nd round of the MLB draft, and today there are only 20 rounds! But he battled through the minors and made the Dodgers' regular lineup in 1993. He was one of the top sluggers of the next decade, with nine 30-homer seasons.

## KIRBY PUCKETT ▶

### Center Field | MLB: 1984–1995

Puckett helped the Twins win the 1987 and 1991 World Series titles, and he led the AL in hits four times and finished with a .318 career average. He was also a 10-time All-Star and won six Gold Gloves.

## BIG
### NUMBER
. . . . . . . . . .

# 396

**The number of homers Mike Piazza hit while playing catcher, the most ever for a player at that position.**

## CHARLES RADBOURN ▶
### Pitcher | MLB: 1881-1891

Pitchers in the mid- to late-1800s threw a lot of innings. "Old Hoss" Radbourn knew all about that: he was his team's only pitcher for most of the 1884 season. He won an all-time record 60 games in 678.2 innings (which is surprisingly *not* the all-time record).

## ◀ TIM RAINES
### Left Field | MLB: 1979–200

With the Montreal Expos, Raines led the NL in steals four times. He had 70 or more thefts in each of those seasons and in two others. A dependable hitter for most of his lon career, he was the 1986 NL batting champ and a seven-time All-Star.

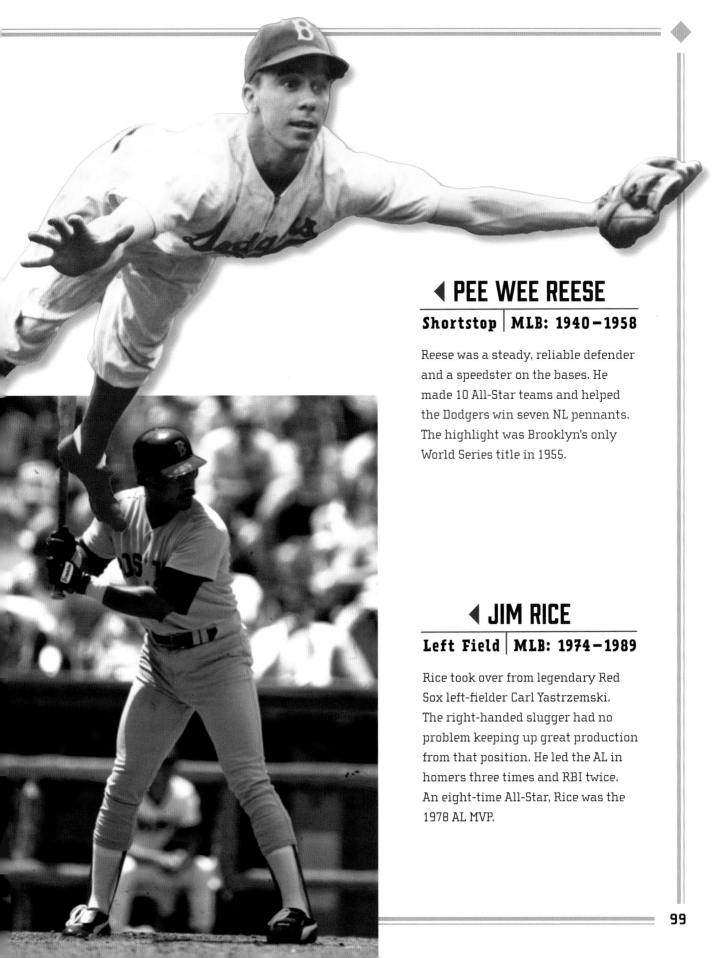

## ◀ PEE WEE REESE

### Shortstop │ MLB: 1940–1958

Reese was a steady, reliable defender and a speedster on the bases. He made 10 All-Star teams and helped the Dodgers win seven NL pennants. The highlight was Brooklyn's only World Series title in 1955.

## ◀ JIM RICE

### Left Field │ MLB: 1974–1989

Rice took over from legendary Red Sox left-fielder Carl Yastrzemski. The right-handed slugger had no problem keeping up great production from that position. He led the AL in homers three times and RBI twice. An eight-time All-Star, Rice was the 1978 AL MVP.

**September 6, 1995:** Cal Ripken Jr. plays in his 2,131st game in a row. That broke the record set in 1939 by Lou Gehrig.

# CAL RIPKEN JR. ▶

**Shortstop** | **MLB: 1981–2001**

Ripken played 2,632 games in a row—that's more than 16 seasons' worth of games! Of course, you have to play really well and be tough to do that. A 19-time All-Star, Ripken was a solid hitter, became a two-time AL MVP, and had eight 25-homer seasons.

## ◀ MARIANO RIVERA
### Pitcher | MLB: 1995–2013

Rivera is baseball's all-time saves leader (with 652). He was also a rare reliever to win MVPs in the All-Star Game, ALCS, and World Series. His 42 saves in postseason play (including 11 in World Series games) are the most ever by far. He helped the Yankees win five World Series.

## ROBIN ROBERTS ▶
### Pitcher | MLB: 1948–1966

Roberts has a bunch of firsts on his Hall of Fame resume. In 1950, he became the first 20-game winner for the Phillies since 1917. That year, he helped the team win an NL pennant. Roberts was also first all-time for most home runs allowed (505), until Jamie Moyer topped him in 2010. But he also walked fewer than two batters a game for his career.

## ◀ BROOKS ROBINSON

### Third Base | MLB: 1955–1977

An All-Star from 1960 to 1974, Robinson thrilled Orioles fans and frustrated opponents. His most famous plays came in big moments, including three during Baltimore's 1970 World Series win. He also helped them win the Series in 1966. He led the AL in ribbies in 1964 when he also won the MVP.

## "IN OTHER WORDS"

Or should we say, "In Other Letters"? OPS stands for on-base percentage plus slugging percentage. Add those two marks to create a new number that shows a player's overall hitting skills of power and getting on base. 1.000 is a great OPS number. Babe Ruth's 1.164 is the all-time best.

## ◀ FRANK ROBINSON

### Outfield | MLB: 1956–1976

Before OPS was a thing in baseball, Robinson was a master. A .294 career hitter, he was also one of baseball's best sluggers for two decades. He cracked 586 homers and had eleven 30-homer seasons. The first came in 1956, when he set an NL rookie record with the Reds and became Rookie of the Year. Another came in 1961, when he was NL MVP. His eighth came in 1966, when he won the Triple Crown and the AL MVP with the Orioles.

# 42

It's not a "big" number, but there is none bigger in baseball history. In honor of Jackie Robinson, all teams in Major League Baseball have retired his uniform number, 42. Each April 15, on Jackie Robinson Day, every Major Leaguer wears special No. 42 jerseys as America remembers what Robinson did . . . and all that still needs to be done.

## JACKIE ROBINSON ▲

**Second Base | NNL: 1945**
**MLB: 1947 – 1956**

When Robinson became the first Black player in the National or American Leagues in the twentieth century, he changed America. A multisport star at UCLA, he played in the Negro Leagues before joining the Brooklyn Dodgers in 1947. He was Rookie of the Year in 1947, earned MVP honors in 1949, and helped the Dodgers win their only World Series in 1955.

## IVÁN RODRÍGUEZ ▶

**Catcher** | **MLB: 1991–2011**

No catcher has more than Rodríguez's 13 Gold Gloves. It's baseball's toughest position and he's on the short list of the greatest catchers ever. He was a 14-time All-Star and won the 1999 AL MVP with the Texas Rangers. His veteran leadership helped the Florida Marlins win the 2003 World Series.

## ◀ JOE ROGAN

**Pitcher** | **NNL: 1920–1929, 1937–1938**

Rogan was one of the most dependable hurlers of the 1920s. In various years, he led an NNL in wins, strikeouts, ERA, and shutouts. He wasn't just a pitcher. In 1924, with the Kansas City Monarchs, Rogan hit .396 as an outfielder while also winning 16 games on the mound.

## SCOTT ROLEN ▶
### Third Base │ MLB: 1996–2012

Rolen was a steady slugger for the Phillies and Cardinals, knocking 25 or more homers in seven seasons. At a tough position, he was also one of the league's top fielders, earning eight Gold Gloves. He hit .421 to help the Cards win the 2006 World Series.

## ◀ RED RUFFING
### Pitcher │ MLB: 1924–1947

A change of scenery worked out for Red Ruffing, who lowered his career-best ERA three times during his decade with the Yankees (after moving to the team from Boston). He also helped New York win six World Series, winning seven Series games himself and pitching (with a two-year stint in the Army) until 1946 with the Yankees.

## ◀ AMOS RUSIE
### Pitcher | MLB: 1889-1901

In 1892, Rusie's pitching was so wild that everyone got tired of it. For the 1893 National League campaign, the pitcher's mound was moved from its former distance of 55 feet to its current span of 60 feet, 6 inches from home plate. Rusie put up seasons of 341, 337, and 304 strikeouts in the years leading up to the mound move. Even after the mound backed up, he led the NL three times in strikeouts, while winning more than 30 games twice.

## BABE RUTH ▶
### Outfield | MLB: 1914–1935

When a player leads a league in a stat, the number is in boldface on his career record. No one was bolder than George Herman "Babe" Ruth, baseball's most famous all-around superstar. His 714 homers are third most, and he led the AL 12 times in dingers. His 60 homers in 1927 were the most until 1961. He was a great pitcher, too, winning 94 games while helping Boston win three World Series. His big bat led the Yankees to four more championships.

## BIG NUMBER

### .690
**Held by Babe Ruth, that's the career record for slugging percentage, a way to measure a player's power hitting. Add up their total bases and divide by official at-bats.**

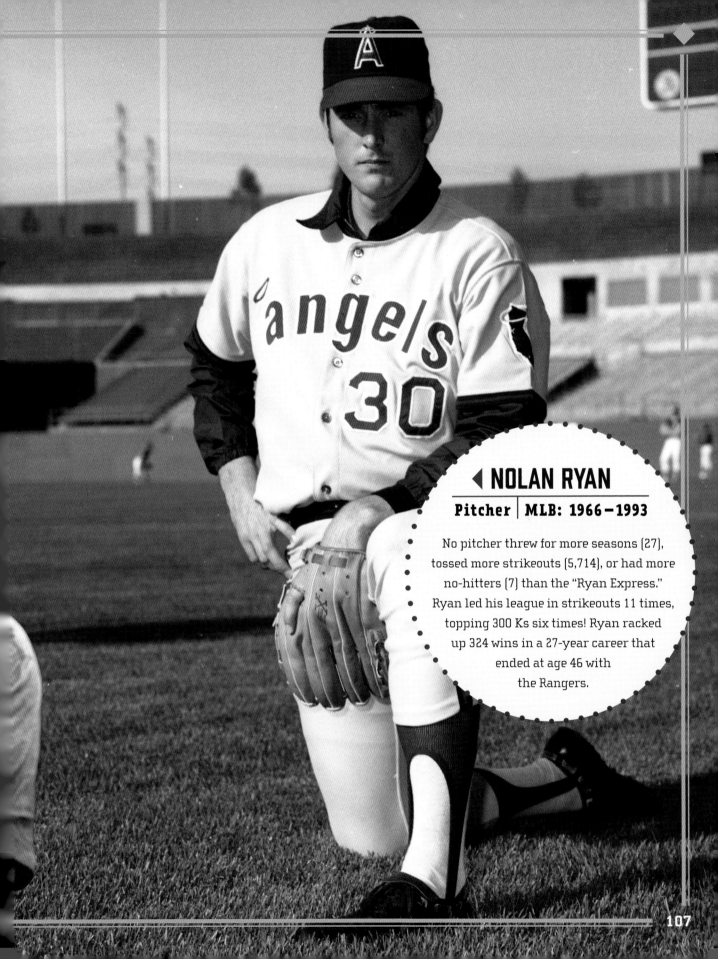

## ◄ NOLAN RYAN

**Pitcher** | **MLB: 1966–1993**

No pitcher threw for more seasons (27), tossed more strikeouts (5,714), or had more no-hitters (7) than the "Ryan Express." Ryan led his league in strikeouts 11 times, topping 300 Ks six times! Ryan racked up 324 wins in a 27-year career that ended at age 46 with the Rangers.

## RYNE SANDBERG ▶

### Second Base │ MLB: 1981–1997

Until "Ryno" came along, few second basemen were not expected to be big hitters. Sandberg broke that mold and became one of the best all-around players of the 1980s. While winning nine Gold Gloves and becoming a 10-time All-Star, he also led the NL in triples, homers, and runs.

## ◀ RON SANTO

### Third Base │ MLB: 1960–1974

Santo's gritty play on defense and a solid bat, along with a second career as a popular Cubs TV and radio man, made him a legend in Wrigleyville. He earned nine All-Star nods in the 1960s and early 1970s, had eight 90-RBI seasons in a row, and also won five Gold Gloves. During it all, he learned to cope with diabetes and later became an advocate for those with the disease.

# MIKE SCHMIDT ▶

## Third Base | MLB: 1972–1989

Schmidt won 10 NL Gold Gloves while also leading the league in homers eight times. He earned 12 All-Star selections, won three NL MVP trophies, and helped the Phillies win the 1980 World Series, the team's first.

## TOM SEAVER ▶

**Pitcher** | **MLB: 1967–1986**

"Tom Terrific" was a standout starter for most of the 1970s and went on to win 311 games in his career. He was the 1967 NL Rookie of the Year with the Mets, then earned his first of three Cy Young Awards as he helped them win the 1969 World Series.

## TED SIMMONS ▶

### Catcher | MLB: 1968–1988

A catcher who can hit is rare, but the Cardinals found one in the first round of the 1967 draft. After Simmons took over as the starter in 1971, he played 150 or more games eight times, with the majority at catcher, and had six .300-plus seasons. He had 193 hits in 1975, giving him the record for catchers with 150 games or more. He is second all-time among catchers in RBI and hits.

## ◀ GEORGE SISLER

### First Base | MLB: 1915–1930

Sisler was one of the top hitters of the 1920s, topping the AL twice in batting average, both times with an average over .400. He had thirteen .300 seasons on his way to a career .340 average, in the top 20 all-time.

## LEE SMITH ▶

### Pitcher | MLB: 1980–1997

Smith was one of the dominant closers
of the 1980s and 1990s. He had at least
one save for eight teams on his way
to 478 for his career, third all-time.
He was a four-time league leader, and
topped 30 saves in 10 seasons.

## ◀ OZZIE SMITH

### Shortstop | MLB: 1978–1996

Smith was a 15-time All-Star and is
considered one of the best defensive
players in history, earning 13 straight
Gold Gloves. Smith made tons of highlight
plays; any ball hit his way could turn
into a "Web Gem" (a highlight
defensive play).

## ◀ JOHN SMOLTZ
**Pitcher | MLB: 1988–2009**

Pitching at the start or end of games, Smoltz was a winner. He began as a starter for the Braves and was part of 14 NL East Division winners and the 1995 World Series champs. After an injury, he moved to the bullpen and saved 154 games in four seasons!

## DUKE SNIDER ▶
**Center Field | MLB: 1947–1964**

The "Duke" of Flatbush had more home runs in the 1950s than any other player. With the Brooklyn Dodgers, he had six seasons with 100 or more RBI, including a league-leading 136 in 1955—the magic season in which the Brooklyn Dodgers took home the World Series title for the first and only time.

## ◀ WARREN SPAHN

**Pitcher** | **MLB: 1942–1965**

Spahn's 363 career wins are sixth best all-time and the most by a lefty. An eight-time NL wins leader, he was also tops in other seasons in strikeouts, shutouts, ERA, and complete games. Spahn was a 17-time All-Star and helped the Milwaukee Braves win the 1957 World Series.

## TRIS SPEAKER ▶

**Center Field** | **MLB: 1907–1928**

Speaker had a terrific .345 career batting average, and his 792 doubles are still the most by any hitter. His 448 assists are by far the most for the position, and he's second in putouts only to Willie Mays.

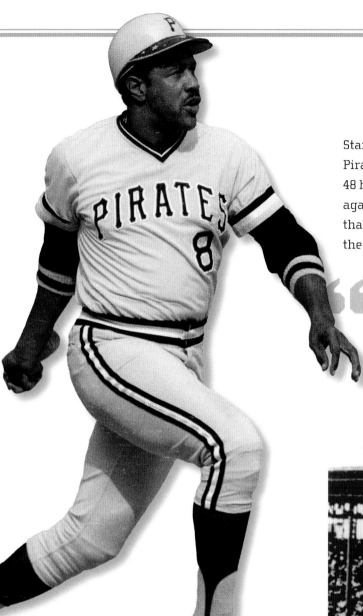

## ◀ WILLIE STARGELL

### Left Field | MLB: 1962–1982

Stargell smacked 475 homers, and he helped the Pirates win the 1971 World Series with an NL-best 48 homers. In 1979, he helped the Pirates win again. Stargell also earned NL MVP honors that year, at age 39, then was the MVP of both the NLCS and the World Series!

### IN OTHER WORDS

**"It's supposed to be fun. The man says 'Play ball,' not 'Work ball!'"**
—Willie Stargell

## TURKEY STEARNES ▶

### Center Field | NNL: 1923–1940

Stearnes was one of the Negro Leagues' best all-around hitters. He led the Negro Leagues two times in average, seven times in homers, and twice in RBI. His .348 career average is one of the highest of all time.

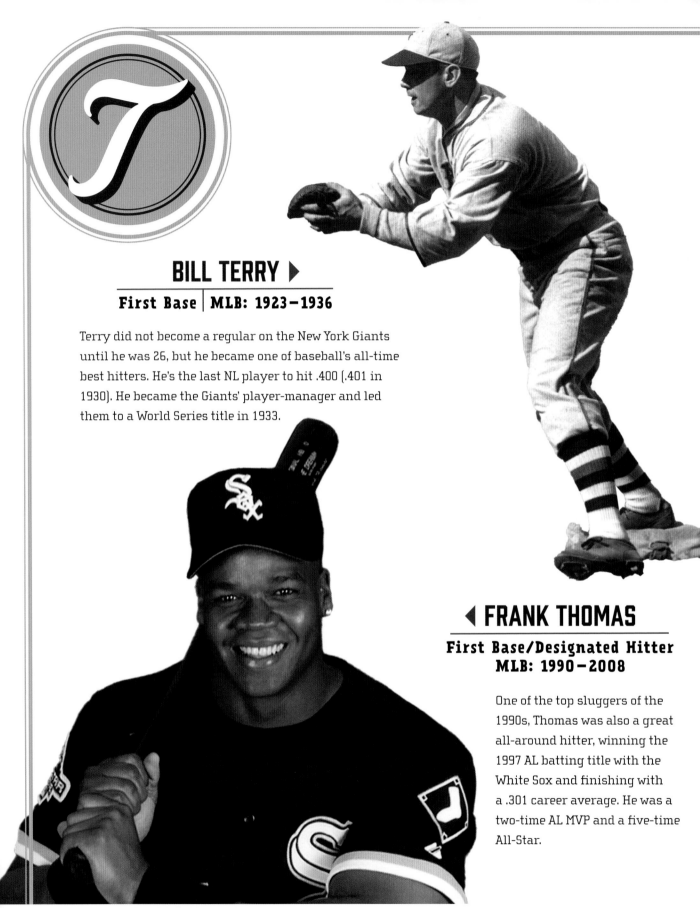

## BILL TERRY ▶
### First Base | MLB: 1923–1936

Terry did not become a regular on the New York Giants until he was 26, but he became one of baseball's all-time best hitters. He's the last NL player to hit .400 (.401 in 1930). He became the Giants' player-manager and led them to a World Series title in 1933.

## ◀ FRANK THOMAS
### First Base/Designated Hitter
### MLB: 1990–2008

One of the top sluggers of the 1990s, Thomas was also a great all-around hitter, winning the 1997 AL batting title with the White Sox and finishing with a .301 career average. He was a two-time AL MVP and a five-time All-Star.

## ◀ JIM THOME

### First Base | MLB: 1991–2012

For Cleveland, Philadelphia, and the Chicago White Sox, Thome had 12 seasons with at least 30 homers, including six with 40 or more. His career total of 612 longballs makes him one of only nine players to top 600. Thome also had 17 postseason homers.

## ALAN TRAMMELL ▶

### Shortstop | MLB: 1977–1996

Trammell was a six-time All-Star and four-time Gold Glove winner, and when he led the Tigers to the 1984 World Series title, he hit .450 and was the Series MVP.

# UMPIRES

**A**long with players, umpires are part of every game. They call balls and strikes, make decisions at the bases, decide foul or fair, and make sure the rules are followed. Here are a few who had Hall of Fame careers behind the mask.

**JOCKO CONLAN:** Conlan worked for the NL for 25 seasons and umpired five World Series.

**DOUG HARVEY:** How much did people trust Harvey, who umpired for 31 seasons? His nickname was "God."

**CAL HUBBARD:** As an NFL player, he won four league titles. As an ump, he worked for 16 seasons. He ended up as the only person in both the Pro Football and Baseball Halls of Fame.

**BILL KLEM:** An ump for 37 seasons, he was among the first to use hand and arm signals and established how umps are positioned behind the catcher. He also worked a record 18 World Series.

**HANK O'DAY:** He did something we'll probably never see again. A former player, O'Day became an ump—and then became a manager! He was in baseball for more than 40 years overall.

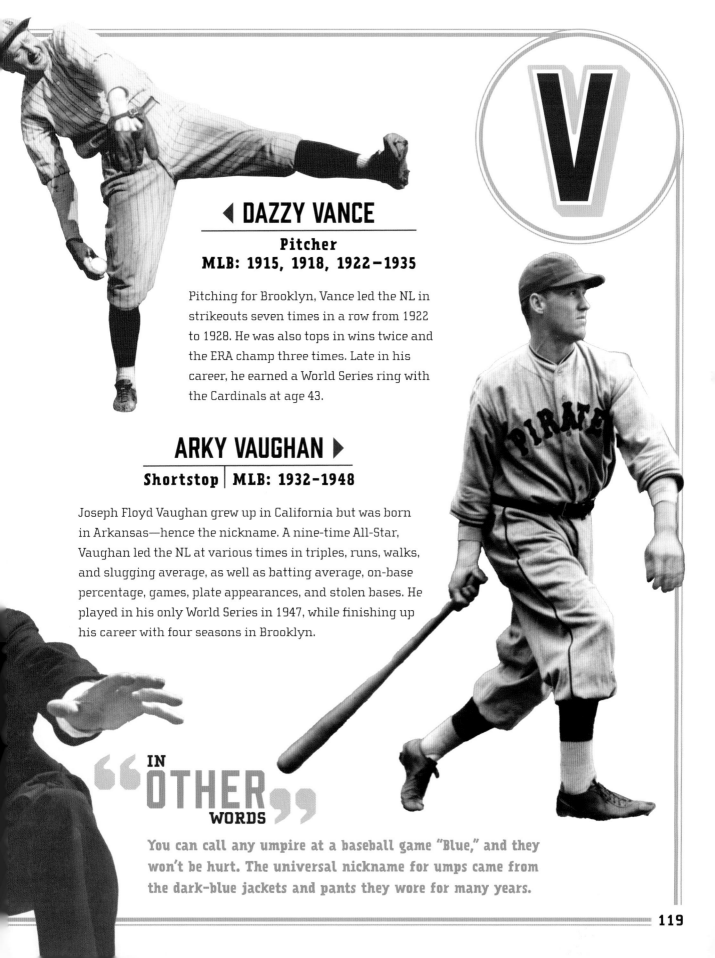

## ◀ DAZZY VANCE
### Pitcher
### MLB: 1915, 1918, 1922–1935

Pitching for Brooklyn, Vance led the NL in strikeouts seven times in a row from 1922 to 1928. He was also tops in wins twice and the ERA champ three times. Late in his career, he earned a World Series ring with the Cardinals at age 43.

## ARKY VAUGHAN ▶
### Shortstop │ MLB: 1932–1948

Joseph Floyd Vaughan grew up in California but was born in Arkansas—hence the nickname. A nine-time All-Star, Vaughan led the NL at various times in triples, runs, walks, and slugging average, as well as batting average, on-base percentage, games, plate appearances, and stolen bases. He played in his only World Series in 1947, while finishing up his career with four seasons in Brooklyn.

## " IN OTHER " WORDS

You can call any umpire at a baseball game "Blue," and they won't be hurt. The universal nickname for umps came from the dark-blue jackets and pants they wore for many years.

## RUBE WADDELL ▶

**Pitcher | MLB: 1897–1910**

George Edward Waddell was one of a kind. Imagine a blazing pitcher who had 349 strikeouts in 1904 (leading the league that year, as well as from 1902 to 1907) . . . and who also leaves games in the middle of an inning to chase a passing fire truck. Just Rube being Rube, one of the best and most interesting pitchers ever.

## HONUS WAGNER ▼

**Shortstop | MLB: 1897–1917**

Wagner hit for power (six NL slugging percentage titles) and stole bases (tops in steals five times and No. 10 all-time). He also hit for average (eight NL titles, tied for most in the NL). His skills in every part of baseball made him one of the sport's all-time giants, and he was part of the Hall of Fame's first class in 1936.

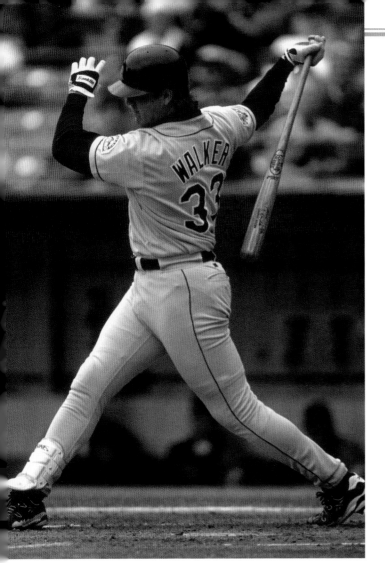

## ◀ LARRY WALKER

### Right Field | MLB: 1989–2005

One of only two Hall of Famers born in Canada, Walker was star in the 1990s and early 2000s. He won the 1997 NL MVP award with the Colorado Rockies and earned five All-Star selections. He won seven Gold Gloves and his 150 assists are in the top 20 all-time among right fielders.

## LLOYD AND PAUL WANER ▶

### Center Field (Lloyd) and Right Field (Paul)
### MLB: 1927–1945 (Lloyd) and 1926–1945 (Paul)

The Waner brothers are the only brothers to both be elected as players to the Hall of Fame. Lloyd reached the NL in 1927 and led the league in runs. He played in the Pirates' outfield with big brother Paul, who was an even better hitter at .333 lifetime. Paul also won three NL batting titles.

## " IN OTHER " WORDS

The Waner brothers were nicknamed "Big Poison" and "Little Poison." But that didn't mean they were dangerous to drink. Instead, the names came from the way that fans in Brooklyn pronounced the phrase "big person" after they watched Paul Waner knock around their Dodgers!

## JOHN WARD ▶

### Shortstop | MLB: 1878–1894

Ward began as a pitcher and led the NL in ERA in 1878 and wins in 1879 with 47. But an arm injury forced a move to the outfield, then to shortstop full time . . . so he hit as high as .338 and led the NL with 111 stolen bases in 1887.

## ◀ WILLIE WELLS

### Shortstop | NNL: 1924–1948

Wells was one of the longest-serving NNL players ever, with 21 seasons for nine teams. He was ahead of his time as a power-hitting shortstop, winning the 1930 Triple Crown while hitting .411. He ended with a .330 career mark.

**September 10, 1933: Willie Wells starts at shortstop for the West in the first East-West All-Star game, between stars of the Negro Leagues. The game at Chicago's Comiskey Park also includes six other future Hall of Famers.**

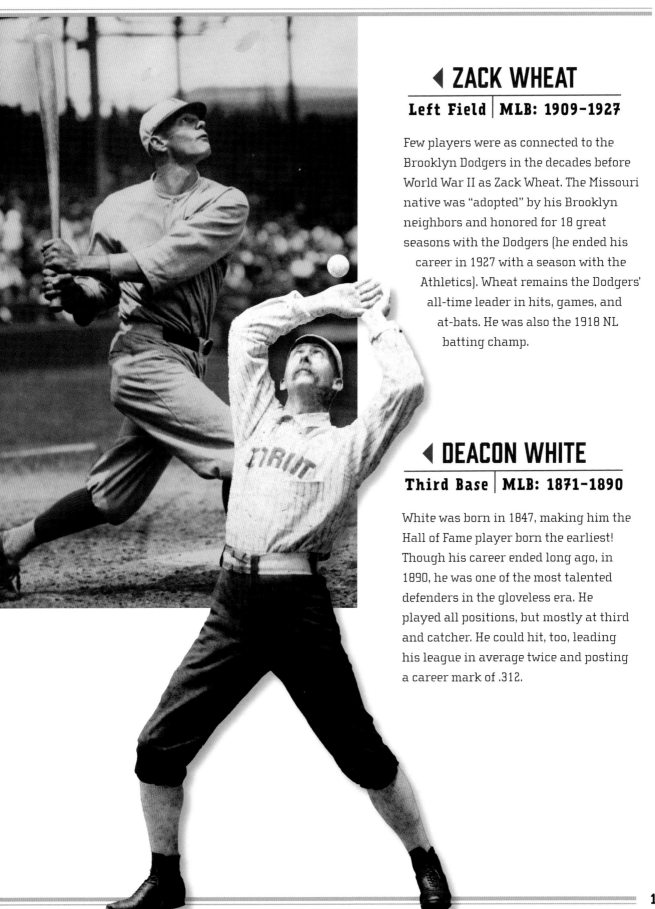

## ◀ ZACK WHEAT

### Left Field | MLB: 1909–1927

Few players were as connected to the Brooklyn Dodgers in the decades before World War II as Zack Wheat. The Missouri native was "adopted" by his Brooklyn neighbors and honored for 18 great seasons with the Dodgers (he ended his career in 1927 with a season with the Athletics). Wheat remains the Dodgers' all-time leader in hits, games, and at-bats. He was also the 1918 NL batting champ.

## ◀ DEACON WHITE

### Third Base | MLB: 1871–1890

White was born in 1847, making him the Hall of Fame player born the earliest! Though his career ended long ago, in 1890, he was one of the most talented defenders in the gloveless era. He played all positions, but mostly at third and catcher. He could hit, too, leading his league in average twice and posting a career mark of .312.

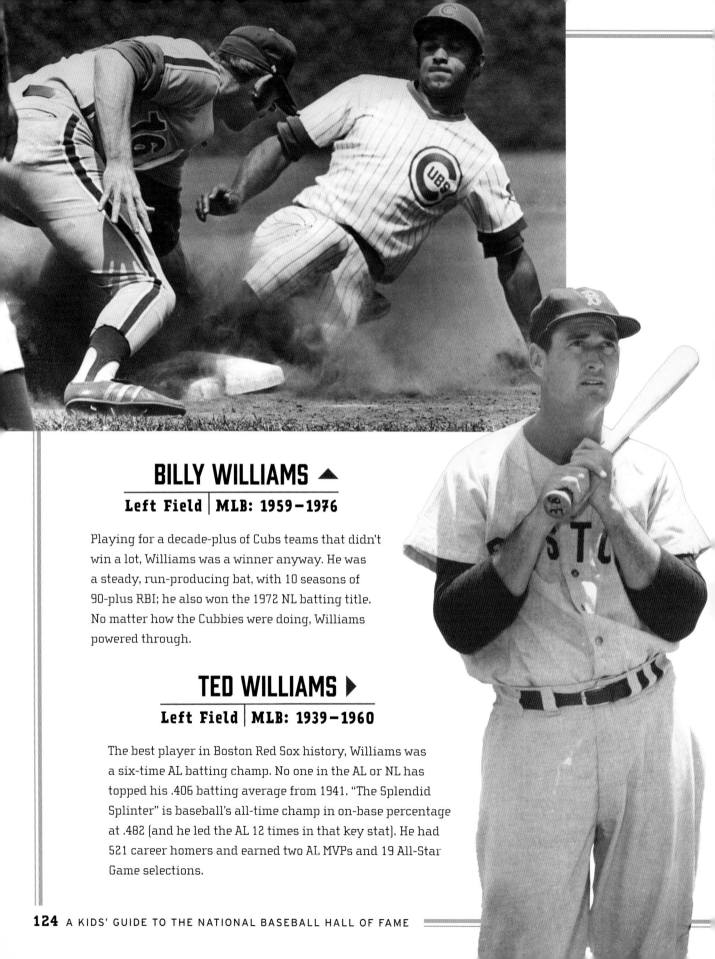

## BILLY WILLIAMS ▲
### Left Field | MLB: 1959–1976

Playing for a decade-plus of Cubs teams that didn't win a lot, Williams was a winner anyway. He was a steady, run-producing bat, with 10 seasons of 90-plus RBI; he also won the 1972 NL batting title. No matter how the Cubbies were doing, Williams powered through.

## TED WILLIAMS ▶
### Left Field | MLB: 1939–1960

The best player in Boston Red Sox history, Williams was a six-time AL batting champ. No one in the AL or NL has topped his .406 batting average from 1941. "The Splendid Splinter" is baseball's all-time champ in on-base percentage at .482 (and he led the AL 12 times in that key stat). He had 521 career homers and earned two AL MVPs and 19 All-Star Game selections.

## ◀ HACK WILSON

### Center Field │ MLB: 1923–1934

Wilson was not that tall, but, wow, was he strong! And that helped him lead the NL in homers four times, reaching a career high of 56 in 1930. He was also a two-time RBI champ, and his 191 RBI for the Cubs in 1930 remains a single-season record.

## ◀ DAVE WINFIELD

### Right Field │ MLB: 1973–1995

A 12-time All-Star, Winfield proved to be a great all-around player, hitting with power and for a good average. His throwing arm from right field was one of the best in baseball. He helped the Toronto Blue Jays win the World Series in 1992.

**Y**

3,308

The number of games Carl Yastrzemski played with the Red Sox, second-most all-time and the most played for one ballclub.

## CARL YASTRZEMSKI ▶

**Left Field** | **MLB: 1961–1983**

"Yaz" took over left field for the Red Sox after the famous Ted Williams (page 124). Incredibly, Yaz nearly matched Williams, earning 18 All-Star selections and becoming the first player in AL history with 3,000 hits and 400 homers. His biggest year was 1967, when he led the Sox to the AL pennant and won the Triple Crown.

## CY YOUNG

### Pitcher | MLB: 1890–1911

How do you get baseball's top pitching award named for you? By being the all-time leader in wins (511), starts (815), complete games (749), and innings pitched (7,356). Young's incredible records will almost surely never be broken. He helped Boston (then called the Americans) win the first World Series in 1903. Fun fact: His real name was Denton True Young.

## ◀ ROBIN YOUNT

### Shortstop/Center Field
### MLB: 1974–1993

Yount is the only player to win MVP awards while playing two different positions. He began as a star shortstop with the Milwaukee Brewers and won his first MVP in 1982 while helping them reach the World Series. He moved to the outfield in 1985 and earned another MVP in 1989.

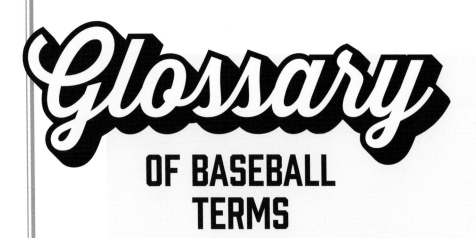

# Glossary

## OF BASEBALL TERMS

### assist
when a player throws the ball to a teammate
who then records an out

### backstop
nickname for a catcher; also, the high net
or fence behind home plate

### box score
a listing of players and stats from a game

### bullpen
the area where relief pitchers warm up
before entering a game

### bunt
a small hit bounced on purpose near home plate

### clutch hitter
a player who often gets hits late in a game
to help the team win

## complete game

when a pitcher starts and finishes the same game

## designated hitter (DH)

only one of the nine batters in a lineup that does
not play in the field; takes the place of the pitcher
in batting order

## double steal

when two players steal a base on the same play

## ERA

earned run average; a measure of how
many earned runs a pitcher allows for every
nine innings thrown

## exhibition game

a contest that does not count in the standings

## fireballer

nickname for a pitcher with a great fastball

## hit-and-run

a play in which a runner or runners take off just
as the batter tries to hit the pitch

## hot corner

nickname for third base

# induction

the ceremony that welcomes new members
to the Baseball Hall of Fame

# Ks

nickname for strikeouts

# longball

slang term for a home run

# mound

the raised dirt area from which the pitcher
throws the ball toward home plate

# no-hitter

a game in which one team does not allow the
other team to get any hits

# on-base percentage

a measure of how often a batter reaches base

# pennant

nickname for a league championship

# perfect game

a complete game in which a pitcher does not
allow a single baserunner (no hits, no walks,
no hit-by-pitch, and no errors)

# putout

when a fielder catches a fly ball, tags a runner, or
steps on a base to force out a runner

## RBI
stands for run(s) batted in—awarded when a batter
causes a run to score for his team

## reliever
a pitcher who comes in after the starting pitcher
is taken out

## save
a stat awarded to a relief pitcher who finishes a
winning game

## scout
a person who looks for baseball talent to add to a team

## second sacker
nickname for second baseman

## shutout
a game in which a pitcher does not allow any runs

## slugger
nickname for a player who has a lot of extra-base hits

## spring training
preseason exhibition games played in Arizona
and Florida

## walk-off hit
any hit that is the last of a game and causes
a player's team to win

# Timeline

## OF BASEBALL HISTORY

**1884**
Overhand pitching is allowed for the first time; before this, pitchers threw underhand or sidearm. Also, Fleetwood Walker played his final season; he was the last Black player in the all-white major leagues.

**1869**
The Cincinnati Red Stockings are one of the first teams to have openly paid players.

**"BASEBALL"**

**1791**
What is believed to be the first mention of "baseball" in America appears in a law passed in Pittsfield, Massachusetts.

**MLB**

**1876**
The National League plays its first season, the official beginning of what is now Major League Baseball.

**1846**
First recognized game played in Hoboken, New Jersey.

**1700s**

**1800s**

**N A**

**1871**
The National Association begins, the first pro league.

**1901**
The American League
begins play, joining
the NL.

**1903**
The first World Series
is played between the
Pittsburg Pirates of
the NL and the Boston
Americans of the AL.

**1919**
The "Black Sox Scandal" hits the
World Series when some Chicago
White Sox players take money
from gamblers to throw games (or
lose on purpose).

**1920**
Rube Foster leads the
creation of the Negro
National League.

**1936**
The Baseball Hall of
Fame elects its first class
of players.

**1939**
Lou Gehrig retires
after playing
2,130 games in a
row; the Baseball
Hall of Fame
building opens
in Cooperstown,
New York.

**900s**    **1910s**    **1920s**    **1930s**

**1914–15**
The Federal League is a
short-lived competitor with
the AL and NL.

**1927**
Babe Ruth hits 60 homers for
the New York Yankees.

**1937**
The Negro American
League begins play.

**NAL**

## 1942

President Franklin Roosevelt encourages baseball to keep playing as World War II begins, to give people something to cheer for; more than 500 Major League players served in the war.

## 1958

The Dodgers move from Brooklyn to Los Angeles; the Giants move from New York City to San Francisco.

## 1959

The Boston Red Sox add Pumpsie Green to their roster, becoming the last team in the AL or NL to integrate their club.

## 1969

Four teams join the National League, including the Montreal Expos, the first team from outside the United States. The expanded number of teams leads to the first postseason League Championship Series.

1940s 1950s 1960s 1970s

## 1961–69

MLB expands from 16 to 24 teams.

16 ➜ 24

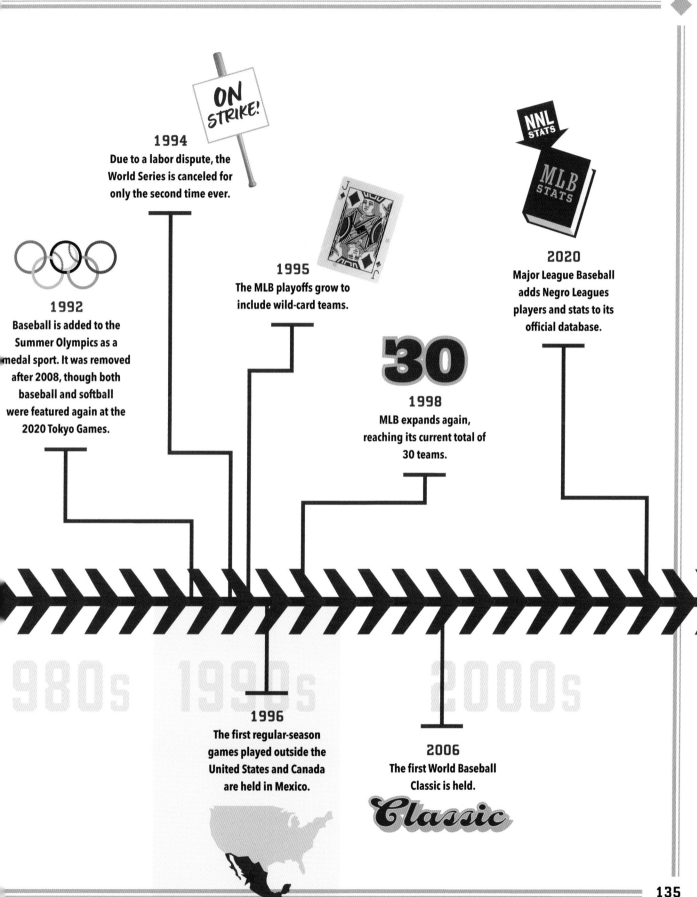

**1992**
Baseball is added to the Summer Olympics as a medal sport. It was removed after 2008, though both baseball and softball were featured again at the 2020 Tokyo Games.

**1994**
Due to a labor dispute, the World Series is canceled for only the second time ever.

**1995**
The MLB playoffs grow to include wild-card teams.

**1998**
MLB expands again, reaching its current total of 30 teams.

**2020**
Major League Baseball adds Negro Leagues players and stats to its official database.

**1996**
The first regular-season games played outside the United States and Canada are held in Mexico.

**2006**
The first World Baseball Classic is held.

# MAJOR LEAGUE BASEBALL

# Top Awards

Each season, Major League Baseball's players compete to help their teams win the World Series. That's the main goal. But some of the star players also shine in other ways. The MLB presents awards in different categories to honor those players. Many of the awards are named for members of the Baseball Hall of Fame! And not surprisingly, Hall of Famers have won lots of these awards.

## Most Valuable Player

*Voted by the Baseball Writers' Association of America (BBWAA)*

This is the big one, the honor for the top player in each league, AL and NL.

## Cy Young Award

*Voted by the BBWAA*

This award goes to the top pitcher of the year in each league.

# Hank Aaron Award

*Voted by broadcasters of each team and baseball fans*

Only hitters can win this award, given to the player with the best offensive performance in each league.

# Jackie Robinson Rookie of the Year

*Voted by the BBWAA*

First-year players in each league are honored with this award.

# Comeback Player of the Year

*Voted by reporters who cover the 30 MLB teams*

This award congratulates players who rebound from injuries, illness, or other things that kept them from playing.

# Trevor Hoffman
## Reliever of the Year (NL)
# and Mariano Rivera
## Reliever of the Year (AL)

*Voted by nine former top relief pitchers*

Having a lot of saves is a good way
to win these honors.

# Ted Williams All-Star Game MVP Award

*Voted by game TV announcers, MLB.com voting,
and the BBWAA*

Chosen right after the All-Star Game, this
honor comes with a crystal bat!

# Gold Gloves

*Voted by MLB managers and coaches*

These awards honor excellence in fielding. Each position in each league has a winner.

# Silver Slugger

*Voted by MLB managers and coaches*

Who needs gloves? This honor goes to the top hitter at each fielding position.

# Roberto Clemente Award

*Voted by the Clemente family, MLB officials, and MLB fans*

Only one player each year gets this honor, given for outstanding community service.

# BASEBALL WRITERS' ASSOCIATION OF AMERICA (BBWAA)

## Rules for Election

## TO THE NATIONAL BASEBALL HALL OF FAME

**1. Authorization:** By authorization of the Board of Directors of the National Baseball Hall of Fame and Museum, Inc., the Baseball Writers' Association of America (BBWAA) is authorized to hold an election every year for the purpose of electing members to the National Baseball Hall of Fame from the ranks of retired baseball players.

**2. Electors:** Only active and honorary members of the Baseball Writers' Association of America, who have been active baseball writers for at least ten (10) years, shall be eligible to vote. They must have been active as baseball writers and members of the Association for a period beginning at least ten (10) years prior to the date of election in which they are voting.

**3. Eligible Candidates—Candidates to be eligible must meet the following requirements:**

A. A baseball player must have been active as a player in the Major Leagues at some time during a period beginning fifteen (15) years before and ending five (5) years prior to election.

B. Player must have played in each of ten (10) Major League championship seasons, some part of which must have been within the period described in 3(A).

C. Player shall have ceased to be an active player in the Major Leagues at least five (5) calendar years preceding the election but may be otherwise connected with baseball.

D. In case of the death of an active player or a player who has been retired for less than five (5) full years, a candidate who is otherwise eligible shall be eligible in the next regular election held at least six (6) months after the date of death or after the \ end of the five (5) year period, whichever occurs first.

E. Any player on Baseball's ineligible list shall not be an eligible candidate.

## 4. Method of Election:

A. BBWAA Screening Committee—A Screening Committee consisting of baseball writers will be appointed by the BBWAA. This Screening Committee shall consist of six members, with two members to be elected at each Annual Meeting for a three-year term. The duty of the Screening Committee shall be to prepare a ballot listing in alphabetical order eligible candidates who (1) received a vote on a minimum of five percent (5%) of the ballots cast in the preceding election or (2) are eligible for the first time and are nominated by any two of the six members of the BBWAA Screening Committee.

B. An elector will vote for no more than ten (10) eligible candidates deemed worthy of election. Write-in votes are not permitted.

C. Any candidate receiving votes on seventy-five percent (75%) of the ballots cast shall be elected to membership in the National Baseball Hall of Fame.

**5. Voting:** Voting shall be based upon the player's record, playing ability, integrity, sportsmanship, character, and contributions to the team(s) on which the player played.

**6. Automatic Elections:** No automatic elections based on performances such as a batting average of .400 or more for one (1) year, pitching a perfect game or similar outstanding achievement shall be permitted.

**7. Time of Election:** The duly authorized representatives of the BBWAA shall prepare, date, and mail ballots to each elector during the latter part of November. The elector shall sign and return the completed ballot no later than December 31. The vote shall then be tabulated by the duly authorized representatives of the BBWAA.

**8. Certification of Election Results:** The results of the election shall be certified by a representative of the Baseball Writers' Association of America and an officer of the National Baseball Hall of Fame and Museum, Inc. The results shall be transmitted to the Commissioner of Baseball. The BBWAA and National Baseball Hall of Fame and Museum, Inc. shall jointly release the results for publication.

**9. Amendments:** The Board of Directors of the National Baseball Hall of Fame and Museum, Inc. reserves the right to revoke, alter, or amend these rules at any time.

## THE ERA COMMITTEES

The Era Committees, formerly known as the Veterans Committee, consider retired Major League players no longer eligible for election by the Baseball Writers' Association of America, along with managers, umpires and executives, whose greatest contributions to the game were realized either prior to 1980 or after 1980.

In all its forms, the Era Committee has elected 181 individuals (115 major leaguers, 33 executives, 23 managers and 10 umpires) to the Hall of Fame.

**Three ballots for consideration have been consolidated into two timeframes:**

The **Contemporary Baseball Era**, consisting of the period from 1980 to present day.

The **Classic Baseball Era**, consisting of the period prior to 1980 and including Negro Leagues and pre-Negro Leagues stars.

The **Contemporary Baseball Era** will split into two separate ballots—one ballot to consider only players who made their greatest impact on the game since 1980, and another composite ballot consisting of managers, executives and umpires whose greatest contributions to the game have come since 1980.

# THE Complete LIST

The following is a complete list of the National Baseball Hall of Fame members through 2024.

## A

Aaron, Henry L. "Hank" 1982

Alexander, Grover C. 1938

Alomar, Roberto 2011

Alston, Walter E. 1983

Anderson, George L. "Sparky" 2000

Anson, Adrian C. "Cap" 1939

Aparicio, Luis E. 1984

Appling, Lucius B. "Luke" 1964

Ashburn, Don R. "Richie" 1995

Averill, H. Earl 1975

## B

Bagwell, Jeffrey R. 2017

Baines, Harold D. 2019

Baker, J. Franklin "Home Run" 1955

Bancroft, David J. 1971

Banks, Ernest 1977

Barlick, Albert J. 1989

Barrow, Edward G. 1953

Beckley, Jacob P. 1971

Bell, James T. "Cool Papa" 1974

Beltré, Adrian 2024

Bench, Johnny L. 1989

Bender, Charles A. "Chief" 1953

Berra, Lawrence P. "Yogi" 1972

Biggio, Craig A. 2015

Blyleven, Bert 2011

Boggs, Wade 2005

Bottomley, James L. 1974

Boudreau, Louis 1970

Bresnahan, Roger P. 1945

Brett, George H. 1999

Brock, Louis C. 1985

Brouthers, Dennis "Dan" 1945

Brown, Mordecai P. 1949

Brown, Raymond 2006

Brown, Willard 2006

Bulkeley, Morgan G. 1937

Bunning, James P. D. 1996

Burkett, Jesse C. 1946

## C

Campanella, Roy 1969

Carew, Rodney C. 1991

Carey, Max G. 1961

Carlton, Steven N. 1994

Carter, Gary E. 2003

Cartwright Jr., Alexander J. 193

Cepeda, Orlando M. 1999

Chadwick, Henry 1938

Chance, Frank L. 1946

Chandler, Albert B. "Happy" 1982

Charleston, Oscar M. 1976

Chesbro, John D. 1946

Chylak Jr., Nestor 1999

Clarke, Frederick C. 1945

Clarkson, John G. 1963

Clemente, Roberto 1973

Cobb, Tyrus R. 1936

Cochrane, Gordon S. 1947

Collins, Edward T. 1939

Collins, James J. 1945

Combs, Earle B. 1970

Comiskey, Charles A. 1939

Conlan, John B. "Jocko" 1974

Connolly, Thomas H. 1953

Connor, Roger 1976

Cooper, Andy 2006

Coveleski, Stanley A. 1969

Cox, Robert J. 2014

Crawford, Samuel E. 1957

Cronin, Joseph E. 1956

Cummings, William A. "Candy" 1939

Cuyler, Hazen S. "Kiki" 1968

# D

Dandridge, Raymond E. 1987

Davis, George S. 1998

Dawson, Andre N. 2010

Day, Leon 1995

Dean, Jay H. "Dizzy" 1953

Delahanty, Edward J. 1945

Dickey, William M. 1954

Dihigo, Martin 1977

DiMaggio, Joseph P. 1955

Doby, Lawrence E. 1998

Doerr, Robert P. 1986

Dreyfuss, Bernhard "Barney" 2008

Drysdale, Donald S. 1984

Duffy, Hugh 1945

Durocher, Leo E. 1994

# E

Eckersley, Dennis 2004

Evans, William G. 1973

Evers, John J. 1946

Ewing, William B. "Buck" 1939

# F

Faber, Urban C. "Red" 1964

Feller, Robert W. A. 1962

Ferrell, Richard B. 1984

Fingers, Roland G. 1992

Fisk, Carlton 2000

Flick, Elmer H. 1963

Ford, Edward C. "Whitey" 1974

Foster, Andrew "Rube" 1981

Foster, Willie H. 1996

Fowler, Bud 2022

Fox, Nelson J. "Nellie" 1997

Foxx, James E. 1951

Frick, Ford C. 1970

Frisch, Frank F. 1947

# G

Galvin, James F. "Pud" 1965

Gehrig, H. Louis "Lou" 1939

Gehringer, Charles L. 1949

Gibson, Joshua 1972

Gibson, Robert 1981

Giles, Warren C. 1979

Gillick, L. Pat 2011

Glavine, Thomas M. 2014

Gomez, Vernon L. "Lefty" 1972

Gordon, Joseph L. 2009

Goslin, Leon A. "Goose" 1968

Gossage, Richard "Goose" 2008

Grant, U. Frank 2006

Greenberg, Henry B. "Hank" 1956

Griffey Jr., George K. 2016

Griffith, Clark C. 1946

Grimes, Burleigh A. 1964

Grove, Robert M. "Lefty" 1947

Guerrero, Vladimir 2018

Gwynn, Anthony K. "Tony" 2007

# H

Hafey, Charles J. "Chick" 1971

Haines, Jesse J. 1970

Halladay, Harry L. "Roy" 2019

Hamilton, William R. 1961

Hanlon, Edward H. "Ned" 1996

Harridge, William 1972

Harris, Stanley R. "Bucky" 1975

Hartnett, Charles L. "Gabby" 1955

Harvey, Harold Douglas "Doug" 2010

Heilmann, Harry E. 1952

Helton, Todd 2024

Henderson, Rickey N. H. 2009

Herman, William J. 1975

Herzog, Dorrel "Whitey" 2010

Hill, John P. "Pete" 2006

Hodges, Gilbert R. "Gil" 2022

Hoffman, Trevor W. 2018

Hooper, Harry B. 1971

Hornsby, Rogers 1942

Hoyt, Waite C. 1969

Hubbard, R. Calvin "Cal" 1976

Hubbell, Carl O. 1947

Huggins, Miller J. 1964

Hulbert, William A. 1995

Hunter, James A. "Catfish" 1987

# I

Irvin, Monford "Monte" 1973

# J

Jackson, Reginald M. 1993

Jackson, Travis C. 1982

Jenkins, Ferguson A. 1991

Jennings, Hughie 1945

Jeter, Derek S. 2020

Johnson, Byron B. "Ban" 1937

Johnson, Randall D. 2015

Johnson, Walter P. 1936

Johnson, William J. "Judy" 1975

Jones, Larry W. "Chipper" 2018

Joss, Adrian 1978

## K

Kaat, James L. "Jim" 2022

Kaline, Albert W. "Al" 1980

Keefe, Timothy J. 1964

Keeler, William H. "Willie" 1939

Kell, George C. 1983

Kelley, Joseph J. 1971

Kelly, George L. 1973

Kelly, Michael J. "King" 1945

Killebrew, Harmon C. 1984

Kiner, Ralph M. 1975

Klein, Charles H. 1980

Klem, William L. 1953

Koufax, Sanford 1972

Kuhn, Bowie K. 2008

## L

La Russa, Anthony "Tony" 2014

Lajoie, Napoleon "Larry" 1937

Landis, Kenesaw M. 1944

Larkin, Barry L. 2012

Lasorda, Thomas C. 1997

Lazzeri, Anthony M. 1991

Lemon, Robert G. 1976

Leonard, Walter F. "Buck" 1972

Leyland, Jim 2024

Lindstrom, Frederick C. 1976

Lloyd, John H. "Pop" 1977

Lombardi, Ernest 1986

López, Alfonso R. 1977

Lyons, Theodore A. 1955

## M

Mack, Connie 1937

Mackey, Biz 2006

MacPhail Sr., Leland S. "Larry" 1978

MacPhail Jr., Leland S. 1998

Maddux, Gregory A. 2014

Manley, Effa 2006

Mantle, Mickey C. 1974

Manush, Henry E. "Heinie" 1964

Maranville, Walter J. "Rabbit" 1954

Marichal, Juan A. 1983

Marquard, Richard W. "Rube" 1971

Martinez, Edgar 2019

Martínez, Pedro J. 2015

Mathews, Edwin L. 1978

Mathewson, Christy 1936

Mauer, Joe 2024

Mays, Willie H. 1979

Mazeroski, William S. 2001

McCarthy, Joseph V. 1957

McCarthy, Thomas F. 1946

McCovey, Willie L. "Stretch" 1986

McGinnity, Joseph J. 1946

McGowan, William A. 1992

McGraw, John J. 1937

McGriff, Frederick "Fred" 2023

McKechnie, William B. 1962

McPhee, John A. "Bid" 2000

Medwick, Joseph M. 1968

Méndez, José 2006

Miller, Marvin J. 2020

Miñoso, Minnie 2022

Mize, John R. 1981

Molitor, Paul 2004

Morgan, Joseph L. "Joe" 1990

Morris, John S. "Jack" 2018

Murray, Eddie C. 2003

Musial, Stanley F. 1969

Mussina, Michael C. 2019

## N

Newhouser, Harold 1992

Nichols, Charles A. "Kid" 1949

Niekro, Philip H. 1997

## O

O'Day, Henry M. 2013

Oliva, Tony 2022

O'Malley, Walter F. 2008

O'Neil, Buck 2022

O'Rourke, James H. 1945

Ortiz, David "Big Papi" 2022

Ott, Melvin T. 1951

## P

Paige, Leroy R. "Satchel" 1971

Palmer, James A. 1990

Pennock, Herbert J. 1948

Pérez, Tony 2000

Perry, Gaylord 1991

Piazza, Michael J. 2016

Plank, Edward S. 1946

Pompez, Alex 2006

Posey Jr., Cumberland Willis 2006

Puckett, Kirby 2001

## R

Radbourn, Charles G. 1939

Raines, Timothy 2017

Reese, Harold H. "Pee Wee" 198

Rice, Edgar C. "Sam" 1963

Rice, James E. "Jim" 2009

Rickey, W. Branch 1967

Ripken Jr., Calvin E. "Cal" 200

Rivera, Mariano 2019

Rixey Jr., Eppa 1963

Rizzuto, Philip F. 1994

Roberts, Robin E. 1976

Robinson Jr., Brooks C. 1983

Robinson, Frank 1982

Robinson, Jack R. "Jackie" 1962

Robinson, Wilbert 1945

Rodríguez, Iván 2017

Rogan, Wilber J. "Bullet" 1998

Rolen, Scott 2023

Roush, Edd J. 1962

Ruffing, Charles H. "Red" 1967

Ruppert Jr., Jacob 2013

Rusie, Amos W. 1977

Ruth, George H. "Babe" 1936

Ryan, Lynn Nolan 1999

# S

Sandberg, Ryne 2005

Santo, Ronald E. 2012

Santop, Louis 2006

Schalk, Raymond W. 1955

Schmidt, Michael J. 1995

Schoendienst, Albert F. "Red" 1989

Schuerholz, John 2017

Seaver, George T. 1992

Selee, Frank G. 1999

Selig, Allan H. "Bud" 2017

Sewell, Joseph W. 1977

Simmons, Aloysius H. 1953

Simmons, Ted L. 2020

Sisler, George H. 1939

Slaughter, Enos B. 1985

Smith, Hilton 2001

Smith, Lee A. 2019

Smith, Osbourne E. "Ozzie" 2002

Smoltz, John A. 2015

Snider, Edwin D. "Duke" 1980

Southworth, William H. "Billy" 2008

Spahn, Warren E. 1973

Spalding, Albert G. 1939

Speaker, Tristram E. 1937

Stargell, Wilver D. "Willie" 1988

Stearnes, Norman Thomas "Turkey" 2000

Stengel, Charles D. "Casey" 1966

Sutter, Howard Bruce 2006

Suttles, George "Mule" 2006

Sutton, Donald H. 1998

# T

Taylor, Benjamin "Ben" 2006

Terry, William H. 1954

Thomas, Frank E. 2014

Thome, James H. 2018

Thompson, Samuel L. 1974

Tinker, Joseph B. 1946

Torre, Joseph P. 2014

Torriente, Cristóbal 2006

Trammell, Alan 2018

Traynor, Harold J. "Pie" 1948

# V

Vance, Charles A. "Dazzy" 1955

Vaughan, Joseph F. "Arky" 1985

Veeck, William L. "Bill" 1991

# W

Waddell, George E. "Rube" 1946

Wagner, John P. "Honus" 1936

Walker, Larry K. 2020

Wallace, Roderick J. "Bobby" 1953

Walsh, Edward A. 1946

Waner, Lloyd J. 1967

Waner, Paul G. 1952

Ward, John Montgomery "Monte" 1964

Weaver, Earl S. 1996

Weiss, George M. 1971

Welch, Michael F. 1973

Wells Sr., Willie 1997

Wheat, Zachariah D. 1959

White, James L. "Deacon" 2013

White, King Solomon "Sol" 2006

Wilhelm, James Hoyt 1985

Wilkinson, J. Leslie "J. L." 2006

Williams, Billy L. 1987

Williams, Joe "Smokey Joe" 1999

Williams, Richard H. "Dick" 2008

Williams, Theodore S. 1966

Willis, Victor G. 1995

Wilson, Ernest J. "Jud" 2006

Wilson, Lewis R. "Hack" 1979

Winfield, David M. 2001

Wright, George 1937

Wright, William H. "Harry" 1953

Wynn, Early 1972

# Y

Yastrzemski, Carl M. 1989

Yawkey, Thomas A. 1980

Young, Denton T. "Cy" 1937

Youngs, Ross M. 1972

Yount, Robin R. 1999

# INDEX

# IMAGE CREDITS

Every effort has been made to trace copyright holders. If any unintended omissions have been made, Epic Ink would be pleased to add appropriate acknowledgments in future editions. All images are courtesy of the National Baseball Hall of Fame and Museum, Cooperstown, New York, unless otherwise noted below.

Page 6-7: © Bettmann / Getty Images

Page 9: © Charles Conlon NBHOFAM (top)

Page 12: © Ron Vesely NBHOFAM (bottom)

Page 12: © Brad Mangin NBHOFAM (top)

Page 13: © Charles Conlon NBHOFAM (top)

Page 13: © Doug McWilliams NBHOFAM (bottom)

Page 14: © Kelly Gavin-Texas Rangers (bottom)

Page 16: © Doug McWilliams NBHOFAM (bottom)

Page 22: © MediaNews Group/Pasadena Star-News via Getty Images (top)

Page 16: © Ron Vesely NBHOFAM (top)

Page 19: © Doug McWilliams NBHOFAM (top)

Page 22: © Milo Stewart NBHOFAM (bottom right)

Page 23: © Owen C. Shaw / Getty Images (bottom left)

Page 23: © Milo Stewart Jr NBHOFAM (top right, middle left)

Page 23: © Media News group Getty (top left)

Page 33: © Bettmann / Getty Images (background)

Page 34: © Michael Ponzini NBHOFAM (left)

Page 41: © Milo Stewart Jr NBHOFAM (top left)

Page 42: © Milo Stewart Jr NBHOFAM (top right)

Page 43: © Transcendental Graphics / Getty Images (top right)

Page 44: © Doug McWilliams NBHOFAM (left)

Page 45: © Lou Sauritch NBHOFAM

Page 51: © Ron Vesely NBHOFAM (top)

Page 52: © Rich Pilling NBHOFAM (right)

Page 54: © Focus On Sport Getty (right)

Page 55: © JEFF HAYNES / Getty Images

Page 57: © Brad Mangin NBHOFAM (right)

Page 58: © Brad Mangin NBHOFAM

Page 60: © Charles Conlon NBHOFAM (bottom)

Page 62: © Bettmann / Getty Images

Page 66: © Focus On Sport / Getty Images

Page 69: © Scott Cunnigham Getty Images (top)

Page 73: © Doug McWilliams NBHOFAM

Page 76: © Charles Conlon NBHOFAM

Page 77: © Ronald C. Modra / Getty Images

# Acknowledgments

Many thanks to the experts at the Baseball Hall of Fame for their insider knowledge and love of the game. The author also thanks the thousands of Major Leaguers and other players who have given him so much joy over the years (okay, a little heartbreak, too . . . but that's baseball).

# About the Author

**JAMES BUCKLEY JR.** has written more than 200 non-fiction books for young readers, most of them about sports. But baseball is his first and greatest love, and he's written biographies of Babe Ruth, Jackie Robinson, Lou Gehrig, and Roberto Clemente. He has also written 25 books in the *New York Times* best-selling "Who Was . . . ?" biography series. Buckley is the author of *The Visual Dictionary of Baseball*, *Obsessed with Baseball*, and the *Baseball Hall of Fame Collection*. He also writes and produces the annual *Scholastic Year in Sports*, where he's forced to include sports *other than* baseball! He coached youth baseball for many years and has helped a summer college wood-bat team, the Santa Barbara (California) Foresters, win 10 NBC World Series national championships since 2006.

First published in 2024 by becker&mayer! kids, an imprint of The Quarto Group,
142 West 36th Street, 4th Floor, New York, NY 10018, USA
(212) 779-4972  www.Quarto.com

becker&mayer! kids titles are also available at discount for retail, wholesale, promotional, and bulk purchase. For details, contact the Special Sales Manager by email at specialsales@quarto.com or by mail at The Quarto Group, Attn: Special Sales Manager, 100 Cummings Center Suite 265D, Beverly, MA 01915 USA.

10 9 8 7 6 5 4 3 2 1

ISBN: 978-0-76038-836-5

Digital edition published in 2024
eISBN: 978-0-76038-837-2

Library of Congress Control Number: 2024932510

Group Publisher: Rage Kindelsperger
Editorial Director: Lori Burke
Creative Director: Laura Drew
Managing Editor: Cara Donaldson
Editor: Katie McGuire
Cover and Interior Design: Brad Norr Design

Printed in China

LEXILE

Lexile® 1060L